MODELER'S GUIDE TO REALISTIC

Painting
& Finishing

Compiled by Jeff Wilson

KALMBACH
BOOKS

Printed in the United States of America

06 07 08 09 10 11 12 13 14   10 9 8 7 6 5 4 3 2 1

Visit our Web site at
http://kalmbachbooks.com
Secure online ordering available

Publisher's Cataloging-In-Publication Data
(Prepared by The Donohue Group, Inc.)

Modeler's guide to realistic painting & finishing / compiled by Jeff Wilson.

  p.: ill. ; cm.

  ISBN-13: 978-0-89024-391-6
  ISBN-10: 0-89024-391-3
  "The material in this book first appeared as articles in FineScale Modeler magazine."

1. Models and modelmaking. 2. Models and modelmaking—Handbooks, manuals, etc.
3. Painting. 4. Paint. I. Wilson, Jeff, 1964– . II. Title. III. Title: Realistic painting & finishing
IV. Title: FineScale Modeler.

TT154 .M63 2006
745.592/8

The material in this book has previously appeared as articles in *FineScale Modeler* magazine.

Contents

Introduction

Making models isn't what it used to be. Decades ago, before plastic models came along, the challenge of the hobby was carving wood to resemble the real thing, but in a manageable miniature size. Injection-molded plastic kits appeared in the 1950s, and over the past half century, the quality of the kits has soared. What used to be ill-fitting plastic blobs have now become miniature masterpieces that possess incredible detail and accuracy.

Many modern plastic kits are more than plastic. Top-end kits sometimes include photoetched, chemically milled metal parts, a few feature cold-cast urethane resin pieces—whatever medium necessary to produce the best detail. Why? Because modelers keep demanding more and more detail. The manufacturers have listened, and now hobbyists expect near perfect fit, accuracy, and detail right inside the box. When you can't get it in the kit, you've come to depend on a burgeoning aftermarket for resin detail sets, conversions, and alternate decals to improve and customize every model.

So what's left for you to do? The challenge of the modeling hobby now is in the finishing: painting, decaling, and weathering. That's what this book is about: helping you paint multicolor camouflage schemes on a tank, add flair to that hot rod, or produce sea-and-sun affects on your jet fighter.

The book will help you, I'm certain. But just reading the book will not transform your hobby. Practice the techniques you find inside the cover. You probably won't attain perfection on the first try, even when you've followed the author's guidelines to the letter. Try out a new trick on an old junker model first. Work on several small models until you feel comfortable and confident.

Practice is even more important with the airbrush. Most modelers have a love/hate relationship with their airbrush. I've known some modelers who switch airbrush brands often, thinking that a different one will make their painting better. But if they practice enough, they find the crucial element is not the brush but the hand that guides it. If you have had trouble with your airbrush, experiment with paint brands, thinners, mixing ratios, air-pressure settings, and spraying distances. Pretty soon, you'll be able to produce flawless paint jobs.

I've been modeling for 50 years, and I still learn with every project. But the lessons I've learned in the past help me avoid finishing problems now. That's the way it will be with you, too. Practice. The more models you make, the easier—and the better—each will become.

Paul Boyer
FineScale Modeler *magazine*

Working with CLEAR PARTS

Make them easier to handle with these essential techniques

BY MATTHEW USHER / PHOTOS BY JIM FORBES

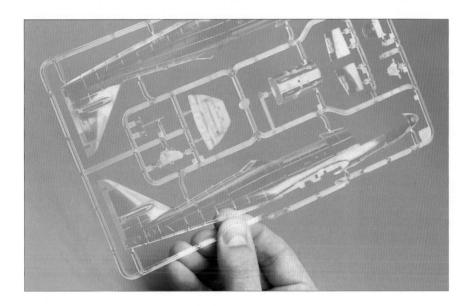

F or a long time, clear model parts drove me crazy. A scratched canopy or a glue-hazed windshield would ruin my enthusiasm for a modeling project because they were problems I didn't know how to avoid or fix.

Unlike the rest of the kit parts, clear plastic is brittle and scratches easily, and you can't hide your mistakes (like scratches or glue smudges) under a coat of paint.

It doesn't have to be that way. Most of the tools for handling clear parts are probably already on your workbench, and adding a few more items will make working with them—and correcting any problems—immeasurably easier.

You might think paint makes a good cover-up. But paint accentuates flaws. So before you paint your model, do everything you can to make the surface perfect.

TRIMMING

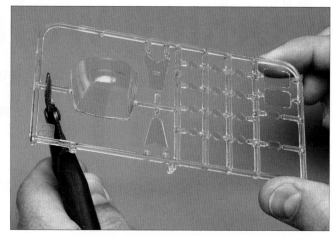

Clear styrene cracks easily, so special care is necessary when removing parts from the trees. A few basic tools—including a parts cutter, a sharp hobby knife, and a few sanding sticks—are all you'll need.

Start by removing the part from the tree. Use the parts cutter and cut the sprue well away from the clear part you're removing. This will keep cracks away from the part.

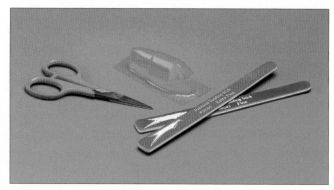

Using a hobby knife with a new blade, carefully trim the attachment stub until very little is left on the part. Work slowly, and remove the plastic a little at a time.

Finally, sanding with the edge of a fine-grit sanding stick will remove the last of the part's attachment stub.

Vacuum-formed canopies are exceptionally thin and must be cut from a clear-plastic sheet before you attach them to the model. Start by carefully trimming the canopy away with a sharp pair of scissors. Remove the plastic a little bit at a time, and test-fit the canopy on the model frequently as you work. A fine-grit sanding stick will help with the final shaping. Reinforcing the canopy from the inside with a lump of Silly Putty will make it easier to handle and keep you from accidentally crushing it while you work.

FIXING SCUFFS AND SCRATCHES

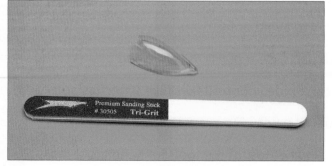

The cockpit and canopy area is one of the focal points of any aircraft model. A scratched canopy like this can ruin your model's appearance.

The solution? A polishing stick, like this one from Squadron Mail Order (No. 30505). The stick has three progressively finer polishing grits that will remove the scratch and restore the original appearance.

The darkest section of this stick is the coarsest. Sanding in small circles will remove the scratch and give the canopy a hazy appearance. Don't worry—you haven't ruined it!

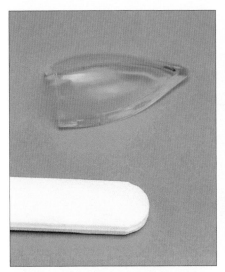

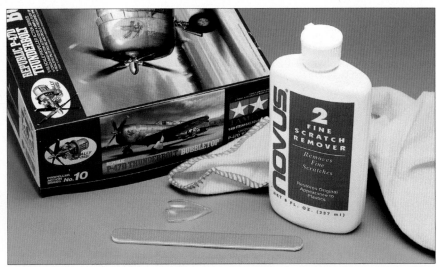

Moving to the middle grit is the next step—it will smooth the sanded area even more and restore some of the canopy's transparency. You're almost there!

The stick's finest grit, usually on the opposite side, is next. Buffing the part with it should remove the remaining haze and restore the part to its original appearance. Polishing the canopy with Novus No. 2 plastic polish (on a clean, soft cloth) as a final step will bring out a brilliant shine.

OTHER TIPS

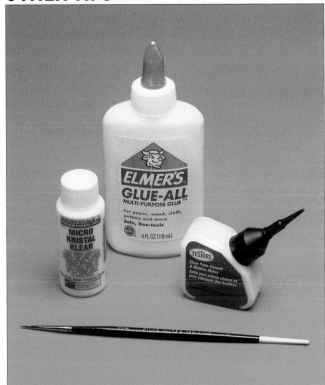

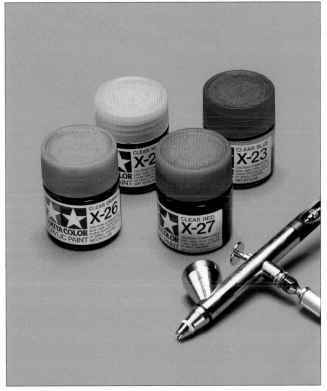

The typical modeling glues you have on hand aren't always the best choice for clear plastic parts—super glue can fog the parts with an almost impossible-to-remove white haze, and solvent cements can mar (and even distort) clear parts. Water-based adhesives like Microscale Micro Kristal Klear, Elmer's Glue-All, and Testor's Clear Parts Cement are remarkably strong, yet won't damage clear parts. If you make a mistake or apply too much glue, you can clean up with water and try again.

Translucent paints (such as Tamiya's acrylics) can be used to tint clear plastic parts. Applied with an airbrush, they're great for realistically simulating tinted canopies, automotive taillights, position lights, vision blocks, and other similar parts.

Sanding tool
ROUNDUP

Sanding is a dirty job, but we all have to do it

BY PAUL BOYER / PHOTOS BY JIM FORBES

Ssshh, ssshh, ssshh, ssshh. Scratch, scratch, scratch, scratch. Voopah, voopah, voopah, voopah. Ah, the sounds of a modeler hard at work, sanding and filing seams and other lumps and bumps off the next masterpiece! Like it or not, we all have to sand even the best-fitting models. Sometimes done just a little, sometimes an awful lot, sanding is an unavoidable step in the modeling process.

When I started modeling, I didn't even know what sandpaper was. I just built the kits right out of the box (usually within an hour or so), used tube glue, didn't use paint, and I was happy. When I got serious about it, I realized that seams made models look like toys and not like scale replicas.

Sanding isn't just for reducing filled seams. It can also be used to dress mating surfaces to make them fit better (and maybe eliminate the need for filler) and to shape parts to the proper contour.

The evolution of sandpaper. Back in the 1970s, there was little choice of sanding tools. Hardware store sandpaper was all that was available. The wet-or-dry variety was, and still is, the best kind. I regularly buy 220-, 400-, and 600-grit 3M wet-or-dry sandpaper sheets from the local hardware store, **1**. You can sand anything with it, and you can also cut a strip from the sheet and anchor it (with glue or double-sided tape) to an eraser to make a miniature sanding block, **2**.

In most cases, wet sanding is preferable to dry sanding. Water keeps the grit from clogging, and that makes the sandpaper more efficient. Make sure the paper is made for wet sanding (it's usually dark gray in color), or you will have a soggy mess on your hands.

The next advancement in sandpaper was Mylar-backed sanding film. Instead of the grit being applied to paper, it is applied to thin plastic, **3**. The flexible material conforms better to surfaces, and the Mylar resists clogging the grit with sanding dust. Wet sanding sometimes causes the grit to part company with the Mylar, though.

I use a full sheet of 320-grit sandpaper laid on a flat surface to dress the edges of kit parts, especially those from vacuum-formed kits, **4**. The flat surface helps provide even sanding of the part, but you have to apply even pressure as you sand. Don't press too hard. That may distort the part and cause uneven results.

Sanding tools. One of the handiest sanding tools to come along is Creations Unlimited's Flex-I-File. It's an aluminum bow that holds an interchangeable Mylar sanding strip, **5**. The Flex-I-File is ideal for sanding curved surfaces where you want to avoid creating flat spots, **6**. The strips can be detached from one end of the bow, threaded through an opening in the part you want to sand, and reconnected to the bow. This way, you can sand the inside of such parts as landing-gear scissors, chassis frames, and so forth. If the ¼"-wide strips are too wide, you can cut them down to make them fit.

Creations Unlimited also makes Flex-I-File Flex-Pads (known generically

1 Hardware store wet-or-dry sandpaper is a basic necessity for everyone's model workbench.

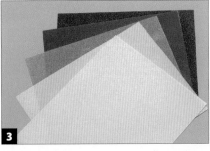

2 A strip of wet-or-dry sandpaper can be attached to an ordinary eraser to make a miniature sanding block.

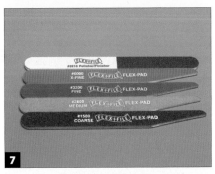

3 Sanding "films" are merely sanding grit bonded to Mylar film.

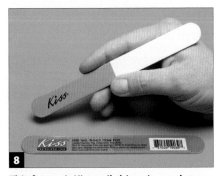

4 A sheet of 320-grit wet-or-dry sandpaper resting on a flat surface is ideal for dressing the edges of vacuum-formed parts such as this aircraft fuselage half.

5 Creations Unlimited's revolutionary Flex-I-File features an aluminum bow holding a strip of Mylar sanding film.

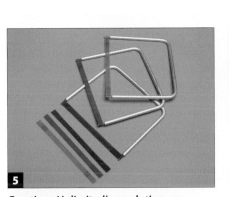

6 The Flex-I-File is ideal for sanding curved surfaces—it won't create a flat spot.

7 Flex-I-File Flex-Pads are good tools for many sanding needs. From top: Polisher/Finisher (three grits), extra-fine, fine, medium, and coarse. The tapered tips allow sanding in tight corners.

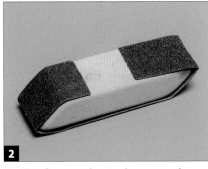

8 This four-grit Kiss nail shiner is another example of a sanding stick. It has medium, fine, extra-fine, and polishing grits. Look for it in the nail-care section of your local drugstore.

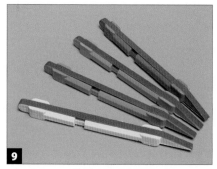

9

Sanding "wands" hold loops of sandpaper that can be rolled like tank treads to provide fresh grit when a spot wears out.

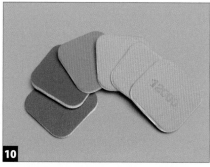

10

Micro-Mesh sanding pads have extremely fine grits for polishing out the smallest blemishes in clear parts and paint jobs.

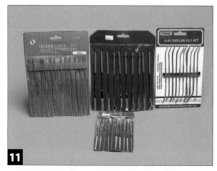

11

Micro-Mark has several sets of jeweler's and riffler files.

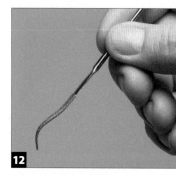

12

Diamond-grit rifflers can be used to file small points in tight places.

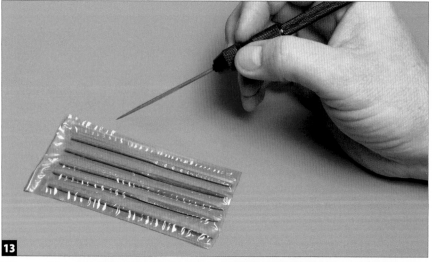

13

This set of fine needle files can be chucked into the all-metal handle.

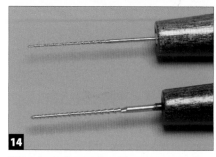

14

Micro-broaches such as these are great for extremely fine work. You can barely see the spiral cutting edge milled into the steel bit.

15

Wet-or-dry sandpaper can be glued to any diameter of brass tubing for a simple sanding tool.

as sanding sticks), which are similar to fingernail shapers. Available individually or in sets, **7**, the sticks come in coarse, medium, fine, extra-fine, and a three-way polisher/finisher that has extra-fine, super-fine, and buffer surfaces. They are ½" wide, about 6" long, and have tapered tips to get into tight areas. The grit is applied to both sides of each lightly padded plastic stick.

Don't be surprised if you bump into a fellow modeler at the cosmetic/nail-care section of the drug store. All sorts of emery boards and nail shapers found there are great for modeling. Many grades of sanding sticks are available, but my all-time favorite sanding tool is the Kiss Nail Shiner, item No. F222, a four-way shaper/buffer with a Kiss label (now isn't that sweet?), **8**. The four grits on this item are labeled coarse (blue), fine (red), Xtra fine buffer (white), and XXtra fine buffer (gray). These are equivalent to medium, very fine, extra fine, and buffer grits on commercial modeling sanding sticks. The Kiss stick is ¾" wide and 7" long.

Micro-Mark's sanding wands are another alternative, **9**. These rugged plastic sticks have unpadded loops of sandpaper wrapped around them. The set of four has grits ranging from coarse to extra-fine. When the grit becomes worn, you roll the strip around the stick, much like track on a tank, and continue work with fresh grit.

For extra-fine sanding and polishing, make sure you have Micro-Mesh sanding pads on your workbench, **10**. The set of six foam pads range from 2,400- to 12,000-grit. They are perfect for polishing canopies and refining super glossy paint jobs on cars.

Files. Sometimes sanding is not the best way to remove material from your models. Consider purchasing at least one good set of jeweler's files. They are available in many types and sizes, **11**. A good set will include several flat, half-round, round, triangular, and square files.

Riffler files are interesting creatures, **12**. They are curved, with grit on both sides of the curve. They work best for filing small points in tight places. Needle files, **13**, smaller versions of jeweler's files, also should be on your workbench. For the really eagle-eyed, consider the two micro-broaches from Micro-Mark, **14**. From a distance, they appear to be wires on sticks, but they have spiral blades that are great for removing material in tight places and cleaning out bored holes.

For rough-sanding tight curves, you can super glue fine-grit sandpaper to brass tubing, **15**, or wood dowels to polish and shape items such as cowls and jet pipes.

Get electrified! Sanding drums and grinding bits can be attached to a motor tool, but there are also a couple more electrically powered miniature sanders available to modelers. Micro-Mark markets two—one labeled Micro-Lux, and another made by Wahl. The Micro-Lux unit, **16**, has interchangeable plastic bits that hold self-sticking sandpaper pads of different shapes and grits. The constant-speed motor vibrates the bits from side to side in a short arc (about ¼"). The Wahl unit, **17**, works like a reciprocating saw—the constant-speed motor makes the interchangeable sanding bits or files go in and out with about a ⅛" stroke.

The motorized sanders can work fast, so be careful you don't get carried away. You may find you've sanded away too much before you know it.

When to sand and when to file. You might ask, why have both files and sanding tools? Each tool has its advantages, and none is ideal for every job. If you want to get a smooth curved surface, a file is not the tool you want in hand. The hard, inflexible file will create flat spots on curved surfaces, **18**. If you want to sharpen corners, a sanding stick or Flex-I-File is not the answer. Because they are flexible, they tend to round off sharp corners, **19**.

So don't let sanding wear you down. Plenty of tools are available to make the job a lot smoother.

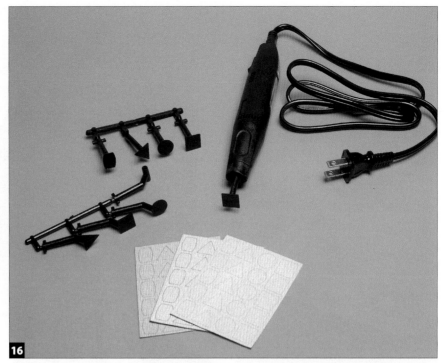

16

More power! The Micro-Lux electric sanding tool has several plastic bits that hold stick-on sanding pads.

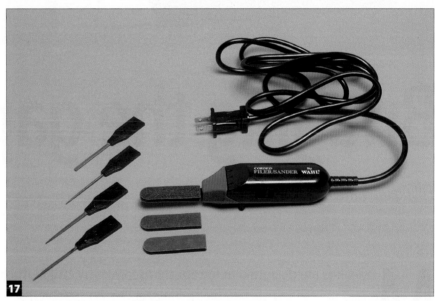

17

The Wahl Filer/Sander has sanding and filing bits that simply snap on and off the unit.

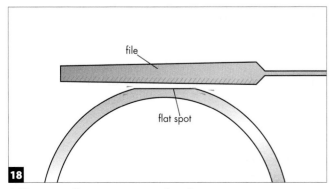

18

file

flat spot

A file creates flat spots on curved surfaces.

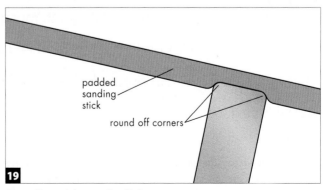

19

padded sanding stick

round off corners

A sanding stick rounds off sharp corners.

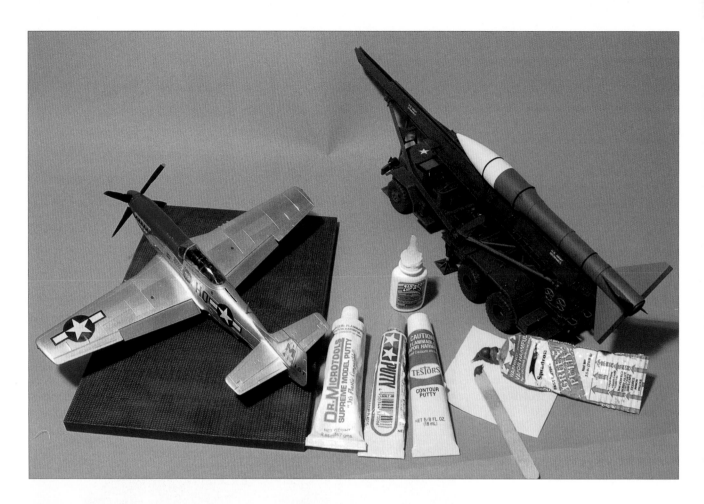

Bridging the gaps

Filling unwanted seams in your models

BY CHRIS APPOLDT / PHOTOS BY THE AUTHOR

Model kits are designed to fit together seamlessly, but in most cases you'll at least need to sand a little to smooth the seam where the parts are joined. In many cases, you'll use putty or gap-filling super glue to blend the joint. Your goal is to hide the "gap" area completely, filling in the empty space to make it invisible to the eye when painted. The procedure varies a little depending on what you use to fill the gap, but as you'll see from the photographs, the results should be the same: That seam will be gone!

ABOVE: Real aircraft fuselages, truck tires, and other model subjects usually don't have obvious and irregular seams or gaps running down their length—an accurate model shouldn't, either. A few extra minutes on the workbench will hide the spaces where kit parts come together.

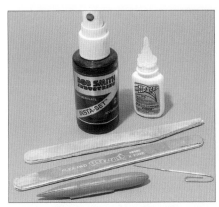

Gaps in external fuel tanks are frequently a hassle, since aligning their halves is never quite as simple as it looks. This gap can be filled quickly with super glue, set in a moment with super glue accelerator, then sanded smooth with a sanding stick.

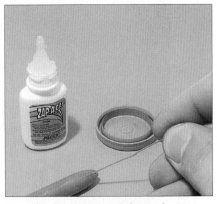

Step one is to use a straightened paper clip or a toothpick to apply the gap-filling super glue to the seam. Soft plastic margarine container lids or film container caps are great platforms to work from—super glue doesn't stick to them.

Putty would work here, but the main advantage in working with super glue is accelerator. Super glue accelerator, applied here with a Microbrush, causes the glue to cure instantly, which lets you get right to work cleaning it up by sanding.

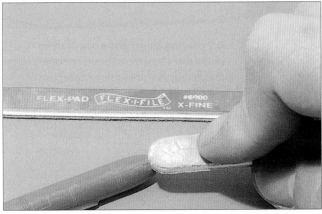

Sanding a filled area with a sanding stick is a good idea because it allows a lot of control over where the grit contacts the seam. You don't want to sand off detail or take the "round" out of your fuel tank if you can help it. Wet-sanding is perfect for super glue. The water will keep the grit particle-free and allow your work to go faster. Just sand it down to the surface of the plastic, and you're ready to paint.

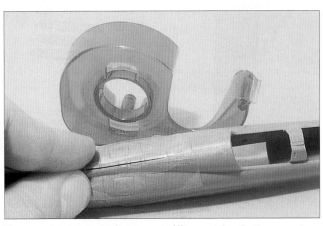

You can also use one of many gap-filling putties. Putty can get messy, though, and end up where you don't want it—try running tape along both sides of the seam so that you won't get it on the nearby surfaces.

Apply the putty with a firm, flat tool such as a popsicle stick. This will allow you to push the putty into the seam and spread it along.

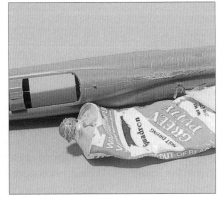

Now that the putty is applied, you can peel off the protective tape. It doesn't look pretty, and isn't supposed to. When it sets (each putty's set time is different—read the labels), you'll be cleaning it up.

Wet-sanding doesn't always work well with putties. Try successively finer grades of sandpaper or a sanding stick to sand down to the plastic. When you're done it will look like this, but after painting it will look great.

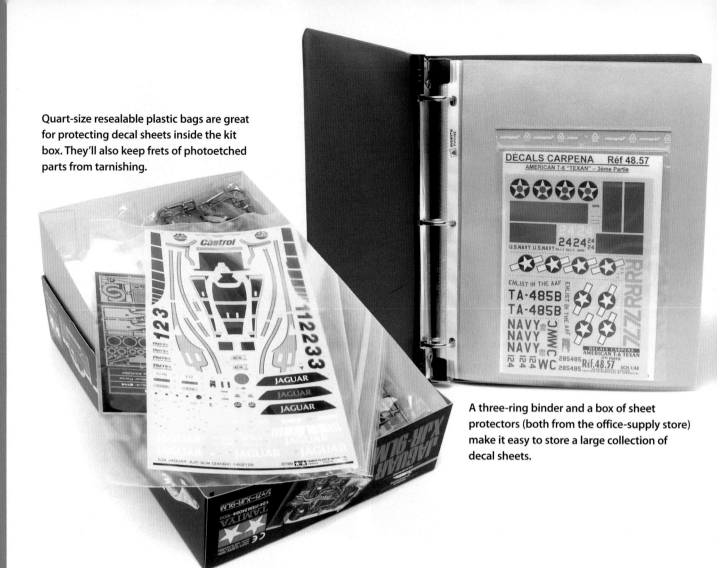

Quart-size resealable plastic bags are great for protecting decal sheets inside the kit box. They'll also keep frets of photoetched parts from tarnishing.

A three-ring binder and a box of sheet protectors (both from the office-supply store) make it easy to store a large collection of decal sheets.

Storing decals safely

BY MATTHEW USHER

If you're like most modelers, you have a supply of unbuilt kits, reference books, and detail parts stashed away waiting for their turn on the workbench. I know I do.

Long-term storage isn't a problem for most modeling products, but some, like decals, require special handling. A decal sheet has a layer of delicate ink applied to an adhesive-coated backing sheet. Stored properly, a decal sheet will last a long time, but if it's exposed to too much heat or humidity it can be irreversibly damaged more quickly than you'd think. The colors can shift, the carrier film can yellow, and the adhesive can go haywire—all bad things for your next model's finishing touch.

So what's the solution? First and foremost, try to store your decals in the most climate-neutral part of your house. The ideal spot will have moderate temperature and humidity levels year-round, so a hot attic or damp basement are not the best choices.

There are workarounds, however. For example, I store my unbuilt kits in an unfinished basement, and to protect the kit decals from moisture, I seal them inside a large zip-close freezer bag inside the model box before I move the kit downstairs for storage. This method protects the decals and keeps everything together in one box, in one place.

I have a large collection of aftermarket decals, too, which I store away from my unbuilt kits. These decals are bound in plastic page protectors I bought at an office-supply store. The plastic pages keep the decal sheets flat, and the sheets are easy to organize by subject or scale. One binder holds a lot of decal sheets and is readily available on my workshop bookshelf. When I'm looking for a new project, they're a great source of inspiration, and the pages are easy to flip through when I'm looking for a specific sheet. Now where are those Farliegh Fruitbat roundels? It's almost time for the Nationals!

Basics of brush PAINTING

Quality paint jobs with brushes are easier than you think!

BY JEFF WILSON / PHOTOS BY THE AUTHOR

O ne goal in modeling is to give each creation a good finish. Airbrushing is often preferred by experienced modelers, but if you don't have airbrushing equipment, brush painting can still yield great results. Brush skill is also necessary for painting detail items and adding finishing touches to a model.

Successful brush painting requires good brushes and fresh paint, as well as techniques to eliminate brush marks.

For the projects shown here, I used acrylic paints: Model Master Acryl and Polly Scale. Both are quality paints that can be thinned (and cleaned up) with water. The techniques for using enamels are similar, but you'll need to use mineral spirits or lacquer thinner. I painted plastic parts in these photos, but the techniques are the same for other materials.

It's essential for modelers to understand how a paintbrush works. Learn how to use the brush and care for it properly, and you may find an elevated status for this basic modeling tool.

Among the author's most-used brushes are (top to bottom) a Model Master No. 0 synthetic, Floquil No. 3 round pure sable, Floquil ¼" flat camel hair, Floquil ¼" flat Silver Fox synthetic, and Model Master ½" flat black sable.

Place a soda straw in the paint, then cap the end with a finger. Move the straw to the paint dish and remove your finger. The paint will flow into the dish.

Brush the paint with as few strokes as possible. Begin new brush strokes in a bare area and gently brush back to the wet area you've just painted.

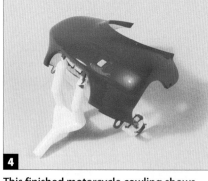

This finished motorcycle cowling shows it's possible to obtain very smooth results with a brush. The attached sprue provides a painting handle.

When painting a rough surface, use a general-purpose brush like this ½" flat camel hair.

Select the right tools. For painting broad surfaces, use as wide a brush as possible. I use round brushes up to No. 5 and ¼" to ½" flat brushes, **1**. The softer the bristles, the smoother the finish will be. For a smooth finish coat, especially with gloss paint, get a good sable brush. A synthetic brush can also provide a good finish, and camel hair is good for rough surfaces and general-purpose painting.

Brush marks are the bane of brush painting. The main causes are brushes with stiff bristles (poor-quality brushes or old ones with bristles hardened by dried paint residue) and overbrushing, which leaves patterns in the paint as it dries.

Preparations. Make sure the surface is clean and free of skin oils from handling. Even a little oil repels acrylic paint, ruining the finish.

Begin by wetting the brush in water (or paint thinner for enamels). Wipe off the brush using a clean cloth or paper towel. This step eases cleanup by keeping paint from drying on the bristles.

Put paint into a separate container or palette—I use an inexpensive aluminum holder. You can use an eyedropper or a soda straw to transfer the paint, **2**.

Avoid painting straight from the bottle for two reasons. First, air is the main enemy of paint, so you must keep the bottle closed as much as possible. Second, wiping off excess paint by pulling the edge of the brush over the lip of the bottle often leaves paint in the bottle threads. This results in bits of dried paint falling back into the bottle, and they will find their way onto the surface you are painting.

Time to paint. Most paints are already the right consistency for brush painting. Thin the paint only if necessary to get it to flow smoothly on the part. Thinning will decrease the paint's opacity, requiring more coats to cover properly.

Dip your brush in the paint, keeping the paint on the lower fourth of the bristles. Brush the paint onto the surface, using as few strokes as possible. Let the paint level itself.

Follow the general direction of surface lines and details, keeping the brush strokes parallel. Apply paint to the bare surface, then use a light stroke to brush the paint back to the area most recently painted, **3**. Keeping a wet edge at all times will prevent overlap marks.

You'll usually need to apply two coats, which is what I did on this motorcycle cowling, **4**. Some colors cover better than others, especially black, dark grays, dark blues, and greens. Lighter colors may need an additional coat. If you're painting white or yellow on anything other than white plastic, start by applying a primer coat of medium to light gray.

As with airbrushed finishes, small ripples in the finish can be polished out by wet sanding. After the paint is completely cured, start with 320-grit and use progressively smoother grades of sandpaper up to 600-grit.

When painting rougher surfaces, such as stone walls, **5**, cheaper camel hair brushes work fine. Since brush marks aren't critical in this situation, you can

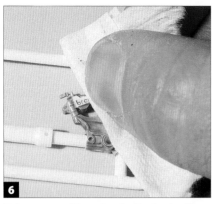

6 Paint recessed lettering its final color first, then wipe the surface, leaving paint only in the recesses.

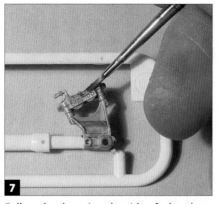

7 Follow that by using the side of a brush to paint the surface around the lettering.

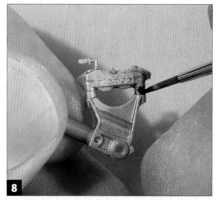

8 Let the part's topography guide you when painting surface details. Using a fine brush, work the paint slowly to the border.

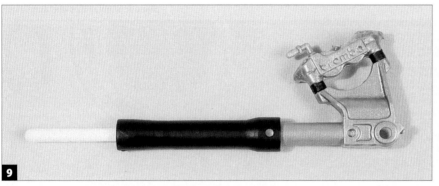

9 Here's the completed wheel fork, with four colors applied.

10 An old mug or glass works well for storing brushes. Be sure the bristles are above the edge of the holder.

move the brush in different directions to work the paint into cracks and crevices.

Delight in the details. My favorite brush for painting tight areas and small details is the Model Master No. 0 synthetic. It has a fine point—finer than many 00 and 000 brushes—and it holds more paint than smaller brushes.

When painting details, start with lighter colors and progress to darker ones, but wait 48 hours before painting one color over another. Paint as much of each part as possible before assembling the model. In fact, keep the parts on the sprues as long as you can—as the photos show, sprues make convenient handles.

Many different techniques are needed for painting details. For example, the motorcycle wheel fork has recessed lettering that needs to be painted red, while the rest of the part must be gold. I started by painting the area with the lettering red, then wiping the surface with a paper towel, **6**. This removed the paint from the surface but left it in the recessed

lettering. I then painted the rest of the part gold, carefully using the side of the brush to paint around the letters, **7**. For raised lettering or details, do the opposite: paint the whole area the appropriate color, then use the side of the brush to lightly dab or sweep across the details.

Let the ridges and relief of the part guide the brush, **8**. With a fine brush you'll be able to work the paint to and around raised and recessed details. If you get stray paint on an adjoining area, don't panic. After it dries, you can either lightly scrape it off with a hobby knife, or simply paint over it with the proper color. The finished wheel fork has crisp, sharp detail, **9**.

Cleaning up. Properly cleaning brushes will make them last longer and help them hold their shape. After using acrylics, rinse the brush under warm running water. Massage a drop of liquid dishwashing detergent into the bristles, then keep massaging the bristles under running water to rinse them.

If you're using enamel, dip the brush in mineral spirits or lacquer thinner. Swish it

around and roll it gently against the side of the container. I keep three small jars of thinner for cleaning brushes. The first is for getting out most of the paint (this is the dirtiest one), the second for cleaning out any remaining paint, and the third (with clear, clean thinner) for a final rinse.

Never let brushes stand in thinner, and never jab the bristles down into the bottom of a container. This can damage the ferrule (the part that holds the bristles) and cause the bristles to splay and lose their shape.

After cleaning, while the bristles are still wet, form them to the proper shape using your fingers (not your mouth). Store brushes bristles up, and make sure the bristles don't rest against the sides of the storage container, **10**. To protect the bristles even more, use the clear plastic sleeves that come with new brushes.

As with any physical skill, your brush-painting talents will improve with experience. Start by practicing with spare parts left over from an old kit, and soon you'll be painting your prized models with confidence and getting show-quality results.

Painting realistic
WOOD GRAIN

Basic brush-painting techniques bring wood to life

BY LYNN KESSLER / PHOTOS BY THE AUTHOR

Most armor modelers have difficulty making wood finishes look realistic. Tool handles, for instance, come off looking a too-even tan; rifle stocks are often too richly red-brown, and again, too evenly toned. Modelers can avoid this problem by learning how to create a wood-grain impression with paint.

Sometimes it's easy . . . Occasionally, items are ready-made for simulating wood grain with paint. Aftermarket resin ammo boxes usually have wood grain molded into their surfaces, so painting is easier. First, paint the box a light wood base color, **1**. When it's dry, give it a dark-brown wash, **2**. I use a standard wash of red-brown and black acrylic paints thinned heavily with isopropyl alcohol, and I use it just about everywhere that a wash is required, from armor to web gear to ammo boxes. The wash discolors the box's surface, and it penetrates the molded-in grain as well.

Dry-brush the box with progressively lighter shades of the base color, **3**, and finish it by detailing the rope handles and applying dry-transfer lettering, **4**. This painting technique will also work for other colors, such as olive drab, and on other articles, such as jerry cans. Its applications are almost endless.

And sometimes it's hard . . . Painting a wood-grain pattern onto pioneer tool handles and rifle stocks is different. Here we have to simulate wood grain using just the paint. It's not as hard as it sounds.

On parts such as pioneer tools, first paint and highlight the metal surfaces, **5**, using metallic paints. Next, apply a tan or middle-brown base coat to the wooden parts, **6**. When it's dry, mix a yellowish shade of khaki, thin it a bit to make it flow more easily, and brush one or two parallel streaks along the length of handle or stock, **7**. Next, mix a reddish shade of brown, thin it, and stroke one or two parallel streaks onto the part, **8**.

To finish the wood-grain effect, mix a chocolate-brown shade of paint and apply another couple of streaks to the part, **9**. Variations in the grain pattern can be made simply by altering your brush stroke; colors can vary, too, depending on the type of wood you want to re-create. To finish detailing the parts, paint their straps and buckles, **10**. You can use the same

1 Start by painting the resin ammo box with a light-colored base coat.

2 A dark-brown paint wash discolors the surface and penetrates the molded-in grain.

3 Dry-brushing with progressively lighter shades of the base color highlights its raised detail.

4 Dry-transfer stencil markings complete the ammo box.

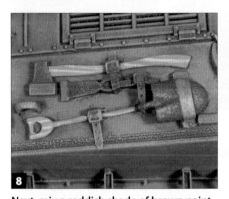

5 On tools and rifle stocks, first paint and highlight the metal surfaces using a dark metallic color.

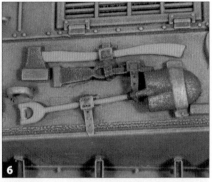

6 Next, apply a tan or middle-brown base coat to the wooden handles.

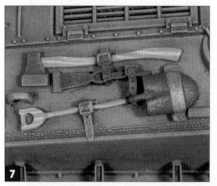

7 Brush one or two parallel streaks along the length of handles using a yellowish shade of khaki paint.

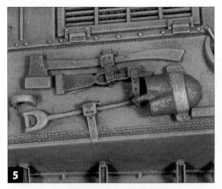

8 Next, mix a reddish shade of brown paint and apply one or two parallel streaks along the handles.

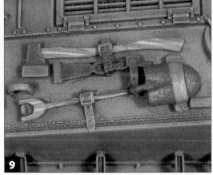

9 Mix a chocolate-brown shade of paint and apply another couple of streaks.

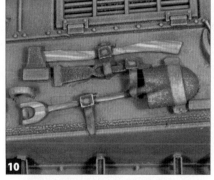

10 As the final step, paint the buckles and straps that hold the tools in place with the appropriate colors.

method to paint rifle and machine-gun stocks, **11**.

Endless applications. You'll find that using these methods both independently and in combination will allow you to create almost any kind of wood grain, from boxes, rifles, and tools to doors, woodwork, and floors. All you'll need is a variety of colors to choose from and photo samples of the wood grain you want to replicate. The only other thing you'll need is a little creativity.

11 The same straightforward painting techniques will work just as well to detail rifles and other metal-and-wood items.

Spray-can artists are out there, many of them tagging the sides of buildings, but that's not what we're after here. With enough practice, you'll gain new appreciation for the "spray bomb" or "rattle can."

Mastering the
SPRAY CAN

Or, how to stop worrying and learn to love the (spray) bomb!

BY MATTHEW USHER / PHOTOS BY THE AUTHOR

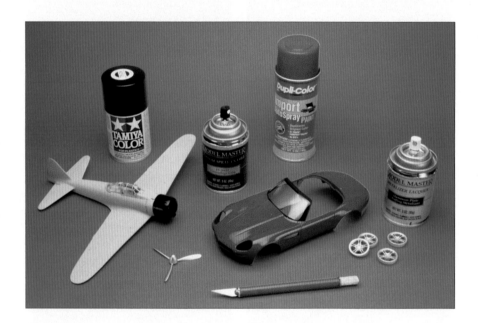

Model paint, particularly spray paint, has come a long way. Years ago, if you visited a hobby shop looking for spray paint to finish your latest project, you'd find only basic colors such as red, silver, and army green. These days, spray can racks feature many shades for aircraft, armor, and autos.

Why spray cans? Most of the models appearing in the pages of *FineScale Modeler* magazine are painted with airbrushes. But don't think that airbrushing is the only way to produce a nice finish. Often, a spray can will paint your model just as well, without the airbrush expense or cleanup time.

Spray cans aren't perfect, though. Although many colors are available, your choices are still limited to just those colors—it's very tricky to mix spray paints. Also, the only control for a spray can is the paint nozzle, which works like an on-off switch. Push the button and the paint comes out—at one speed and in one spray pattern. These drawbacks may put complex, custom-mixed paint schemes out of reach. But in most cases you'll still be able to get good-looking results.

Troubleshooting

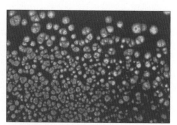

PROBLEM: A rough, pebbly finish.

CAUSE: The spray can is too far away, and the paint is drying in the air on the way to the model.

SOLUTION: Move the spray can closer to the model, and apply the paint using smooth, slow strokes.

PROBLEM: Runs in the finish.

CAUSE: Too much paint! The spray can is too close to the model, or the paint is being applied with an uneven, stop-and-start spray stroke.

SOLUTION: Start spraying off one side of the model, and continue spraying until you're off the other side.

PROBLEM: "Fish eyes."

CAUSE: Surface contaminants push through the freshly applied paint, producing unpainted circles in the finish.

SOLUTION: Clean the model thoroughly with soap and water just before painting.

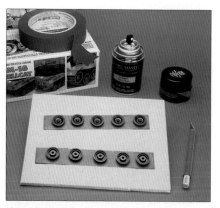

To produce a smooth finish, let the can sit in warm water for a few minutes. Then dry it, shake it thoroughly, and start painting. The warm paint will flow easier and produce a smoother finish. It's an old trick—and it works!

Some parts can be difficult to hold while painting. Find a long piece of sprue, and use a tiny drop of super glue to attach it to the part in an inconspicuous place. After the paint is dry, just pop the part loose and install it on the model.

If you have lots of small parts to paint the same color, attach them to a piece of cardboard with a sticky-side-out loop of masking tape. You can paint all the parts at once, "assembly line" style, and the tape will keep the parts from scattering across the floor.

Getting started. Before spraying, make sure the parts you're painting are secured. The spray's force can scatter small items, so fasten them to a piece of cardboard with sticky-side-out loops of masking tape. When painting a larger part, fashion a paint stand out of a wire coat hanger and tape it to the inside of the model. You'll be able to move it as needed to make the most of the can's limited spray pattern.

Preparing the spray can. Warming the paint can will help the paint flow once it reaches the model, producing a smoother finish. Simply place the can in a glass of warm water.

The water should be about 100°F (38°C), so sink water should be okay. Never heat the water or spray paint can on the stove, in the oven, or in the microwave—the can may explode and cause serious damage or injury.

Let the can sit in the water for a few minutes until it's warm to the touch. Remove it from the water and dry it. Shake the can for a couple of minutes, and make sure the ball bearing inside is rattling freely (this is where the expression "rattle can" comes from).

Painting. With the paint warm and thoroughly mixed, you're ready to start. The trick to applying a smooth, even finish is to use a smooth, even stroke.

The illustration on page 22 shows the correct technique. Press the nozzle button with the can aimed to one side of the model, about 10" to 12" away. Hold the button down and sweep the paint slowly across the model, keeping the nozzle at a constant distance. Hold the button down until you're off the other side of the model. Turn the model as needed to ensure good paint coverage, and shake the can between passes.

When you're finished, move the parts to a dust-free area to dry completely before handling. Placing the parts in a plastic storage container keeps them out of harm's way as they dry.

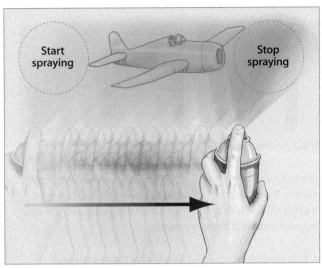

Press the nozzle button with the can aimed to one side of the model, about 10" to 12" away. Sweep the paint slowly across the model, keeping the nozzle a constant distance from the surface. Hold the button down until you're off the other side of the model.

If you want to apply smooth gloss finishes straight from the can, a polishing kit may be what you're looking for. This kit contains several fine-grit sanding cloths (ranging from 2400- to 12000-grit) and liquid polishes that can coax a glass-smooth finish from even the lumpiest paint jobs. The kit is also handy for preparing plastic surfaces for metallic finishes and for removing imperfections from canopies and other clear parts.

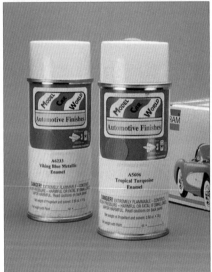

Testor offers six shades of its Metalizer line in spray cans. Metalizers go on thin, so prepare the parts carefully and remove any sanding scratches or surface flaws.

A few mail-order modeling paint companies offer spray paint in factory-matched automotive colors. Some of these paints require special primers, so double-check the directions.

Scale Motorsport's Faux Fabrix textured spray paint has a suedelike texture when dry. If you apply a metallic finish over the textured paint, the surface of the part will look like unfinished cast metal.

A little maintenance after painting will keep the spray can working properly so it will be ready the next time you need it. Remove the model from the area and turn the can upside down. Push the spray button for a few seconds while the can is inverted, until paint stops coming out. This clears excess paint from the nozzle and keeps it from clogging. If the nozzle is covered in paint, dip a cotton swab in lacquer thinner and wipe it away.

Safety. Safety should always be your first concern when working with spray paints. Invest in a good two-stage respirator mask and wear it every time you paint. Spray can fumes are flammable, so work in an area with plenty of ventilation, away from ignition sources such as pilot lights. When you're not using them, store spray cans out of the reach of youngsters, and dispose of empty cans properly.

Summing up. This should help you get started if you're a beginner, or improve your technique if you already have experience. Though they have limitations, spray cans can produce eye-catching finishes.

In some cases, the only difference between an airbrush and a spray can is the ease of use. Go ahead—make it easy on yourself.

AIRBRUSH
troubleshooting

Even after years of experience, you're going to encounter problems when airbrushing. Here's a peek at some of the problems I've run into, and how to solve them.

BY PAUL BOYER

Clouds of paint swirling in your spray area. Whoa! Back off the air pressure and the paint volume. Any clouds of overspray constitute wasted paint. The airbrush can deliver fine, smooth paint jobs, so take your time and apply the paint in thin layers.

Whether you have clouds of paint or not, paint and thinner fumes can be toxic. Make sure you have sufficient ventilation in your work area. A spray booth is best—it can remove all the fumes. A ventilator mask is a good idea, too.

Spidery splashes. Those are the spots of paint with little rivulets running out all over. They have several causes, sometimes more than one at the same time. Usually it means you're too close to the surface with too much paint coming out of the airbrush. Also, the paint could be too thin.

First, close the nozzle to limit the amount of paint coming out, then test spray on your test model to get a feel for the proper distance. If you're still getting spiders, add more paint into the mixture.

Overspray. Watch where you're aiming your airbrush. While you are concentrating on spraying a certain spot, parts of the model that lie behind your target may accidentally receive overspray as you paint. Make sure you mask these areas before airbrushing. If you forget, you may have to repaint the affected areas.

Gritty finish. The paint is covering, but it is covering with small grits and lumps. There are four possible causes: the paint is not thinned enough; the airbrush is too far away and the paint is drying on the

If you've attempted airbrushing only a few times, you've probably suspected there must be mysterious tricks involved. Practice is the only way you will master the powers of the airbrush.

way to the model; clumps of pigment are not dissolving in the thinner; or there is too much air pressure. You don't need to blast paint on with an airbrush—a gentle whisper of paint should be enough to deliver a smooth finish. Adjust the air pressure (if you can) to between 10 and 20 psi, and make sure the paint is well mixed.

Drips and runs. Too much paint in one spot will form a puddle, and gravity will make it run. Keep the airbrush moving so you don't pile up too much paint on one area.

Spatters. Little spatters around fine lines are usually caused by a damaged needle or nozzle. Paint blows off the distorted tip and lands outside of the intended area. Sometimes low air pressure can cause this.

Examine the needle and nozzle with a magnifying glass. If the nozzle is cracked or splayed open, replace it. If the tip of the needle is bent, you can carefully straighten it out. Single-action needles are relatively sturdy, and you can persuade the bent tip by pressing it against a hard surface. Go easy: press, check, press some more, check again, and so forth.

The fine needle of a double-action (or a hybrid) airbrush is more delicate. You may not be able to see the bent tip, but you'll be able to feel it. Remove the needle from the airbrush and drag it lightly over your fingertip. Roll the needle as you drag, and you'll feel the hooked side catch as it goes along your finger. Make note of the direction of the hook, then drag the affected side of the needle on fine-grit sandpaper or a sanding stick. Check it again on your finger and repeat if necessary.

Bleed under masking tape. This is usually caused by too heavy an application of paint. The wet paint overwhelms the masking tape and creeps under, resulting in a ragged line. Airbrush several light coats instead of trying to cover with a heavy coat. Also, spray at an angle over the tape so the air pressure isn't forcing the paint under the mask.

No paint coming out. Shame, shame, you haven't been cleaning the airbrush properly. Most likely some dried paint is clogging the nozzle. Be sure to clean your airbrush after every painting session.

Cleaning your airbrush
BY TERRY THOMPSON

Without a doubt, the most important aspect of airbrushing is cleaning the equipment. Neglecting to clean a brush properly is also the absolute best, or at least the simplest, way of assuring yourself of never-ending frustration while painting.

However, cleaning your airbrush doesn't have to be a chore. I can clean my double-action airbrush completely in less than 10 minutes and clean it well enough to change colors in fewer than five. While I learned most of these techniques the hard way, reading this article means you won't have to.

Single- and double-action airbrushes require different procedures; clean hybrid airbrushes as you would a double-action brush. I've organized the information on page 26 into three categories, one for rinsing the equipment and two for cleaning the airbrush itself. Choose the two that apply to your situation. If you're only changing colors, you can normally skip the disassembly and just rinse, unless you're going from a dark color to a light one, or from a metallic paint to a non-metallic. Then you'll still have to clean the brush completely.

Tips for keeping your brush clean and healthy:

■ Never shake paint—always stir. Shaking leaves paint around the top of the jar, where it dries into clumps. Those clumps can easily clog an airbrush. A screen on your pickup tube can help, as can straining your paint.

■ If you use a single-action brush, close it (run the needle forward or twist the tip closed) if it will sit for more than 20 seconds. Thinned paint dries on and in an open tip quickly.

■ Drain your compressor's water trap each time you spray. It can't work if it's full.

■ Make sure your thinner is clean. Dirt or lint (been doing the old tip-the-can-onto-the-towel trick?) can and will clog your brush, or at least appear in your paint.

■ Lubricate your airbrush according to the instructions, and don't abuse it by overtightening the threads.

■ Some parts—including washers, gaskets, and even needles and tips—will wear out. Paint is abrasive, and solvents are harsh chemicals. Keep spares on hand so you can keep painting.

■ If you think you might have bent your airbrush needle, check it visually or by pulling it across a towel while rotating the needle. Do not check it by running it back into the brush—that just ensures you'll ruin your tip also.

■ If you own needles and nozzles/tips in multiple sizes, keep the sets together. Though they may look similar, they're not interchangeable.

■ If you can afford to, it's a good idea to have separate airbrushes for solvent-based paints and acrylics. The two don't mix well, and paint left in a brush can form clots when exposed to the wrong solvent.

■ When you reassemble a double-action brush, the action should be crisp. If the needle sticks in the nozzle, or if the action seems mushy, there's still paint in the nozzle. Clean it again.

■ If you get bubbles in your color cup or feed jar, you have an air leak in your brush, probably where the tip joins the nozzle. Check your brush's instructions to see whether it can be repaired by the user.

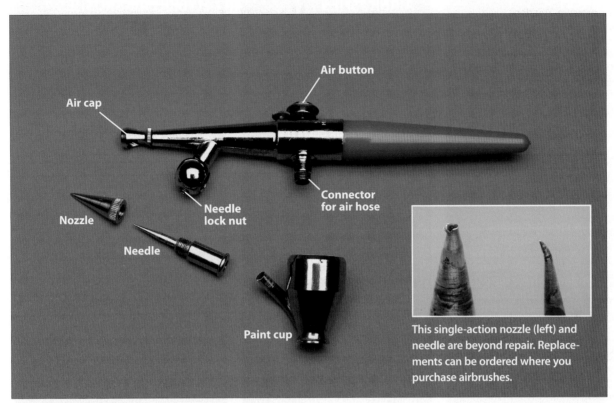

Air button

Air cap

Nozzle

Needle

Needle lock nut

Connector for air hose

Paint cup

This single-action nozzle (left) and needle are beyond repair. Replacements can be ordered where you purchase airbrushes.

Here is the single-action Paasche H broken down for cleaning.

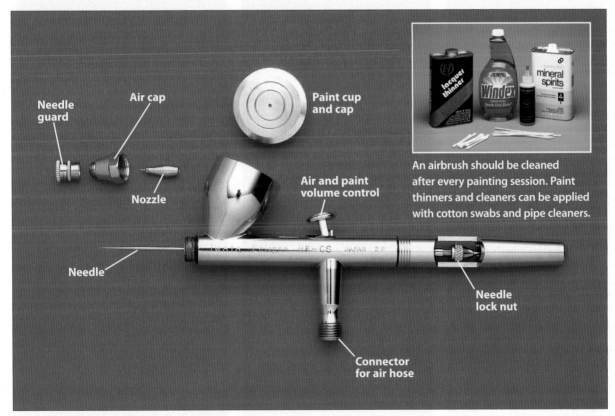

Needle guard

Air cap

Paint cup and cap

Nozzle

Air and paint volume control

Needle

Needle lock nut

Connector for air hose

An airbrush should be cleaned after every painting session. Paint thinners and cleaners can be applied with cotton swabs and pipe cleaners.

This is a disassembled double-action Iwata Eclipse.

RINSING THE EQUIPMENT

WHAT YOU'LL NEED
Mineral spirits and lacquer thinner (for enamels) or distilled water and Windex (for acrylics), Testor acrylic paint remover or other hobby paint remover, paper towels, cleaning station. The instructions refer to both "solvent" and "cleaner." For enamels, use mineral spirits as the solvent and lacquer thinner as the cleaner; for acrylics, water is the solvent and Windex is the cleaner.

WHAT YOU'LL DO
1] Immediately upon completing your painting session, remove the feed jar or color cup. Pour the thinned paint into your waste paint container (never save it) and flush the cup or jar with solvent. If your brush has a non-removable cup, pour the paint out, then flush the cup with solvent until most of the paint is out.

2] Still working quickly, pour the dirty solvent into your waste paint container and refill the cup or jar with cleaner.

3] Spray nearly a full jar or cup of cleaner through the brush into your cleaning station or other container. Let the brush sit with cleaner in it.

4] Remove and clean the feed jar and tube using cleaner-dampened swabs, pipe cleaners (for the tube only), and paper towels. If your brush uses a non-removable color cup, clean it using dampened swabs and paper towels.

5] Spray the remaining cleaner through the brush, then clean the brush (see below).

6] Reassemble the brush, then spray clean solvent through the brush and onto a white paper towel. If it comes out clean, go to step 7. If not, repeat steps 4 and 5 as needed, using paint remover as needed.

7] Spray the remaining solvent through the brush and into your cleaning station or container. If you're using a double-action or hybrid brush, remove and oil the needle, then replace it. Don't leave cleaner, solvent, or paint remover in the airbrush during storage.

SINGLE-ACTION AIRBRUSHES

WHAT YOU'LL NEED
cotton swabs, pipe cleaners, paper towels, cleaner, paint remover

WHAT YOU'LL DO
A] Rinse the paint out of the brush using the appropriate solvent and cleaner.

B] Remove the feed jar or cup (if possible).

C] Disassemble the nozzle assembly carefully. Wipe each piece clean with a swab dampened with the appropriate cleaner solution. For stubborn acrylics that don't wipe off using Windex, use paint remover.

D] Clean the inside of the paint tip (where the feed tube attaches) with a dampened swab or pipe cleaner.

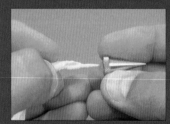

Paper towel rolled into a point helps clean the airbrush nozzle.

E] Twist a corner of a paper towel into a point, dampen it, and clean the inside of the nozzle. Never force anything, including a pipe cleaner, through the nozzle. If the nozzle won't come clean, soak it in lacquer thinner or paint remover, depending on what type of paint is on it. Then clean it using a piece of dampened toweling.

F] Reassemble the brush, then go to step 6 at left.

DOUBLE-ACTION AND HYBRID AIRBRUSHES

WHAT YOU'LL NEED
cotton swabs, pipe cleaners, soft cloth, paper towels, cleaner, paint remover

WHAT YOU'LL DO
A] Rinse the paint out of the brush using the appropriate solvent and cleaner.

B] Remove the feed jar or cup (if possible). Working carefully according to the manufacturer's instructions, remove the needle. (Exception: On Aztek double-action brushes, the needle/tip assembly is a unit. Testor does not recommend disassembling it, so just flush or soak it until clean).

C] Disassemble the nozzle assembly carefully. Wipe each piece clean with a swab dampened with the appropriate cleaner solution. For stubborn acrylics that don't wipe off with Windex, use the Testor paint remover.

D] Clean the inside of the paint tip (where the feed tube attaches) with a cleaner-dampened swab or pipe cleaner. If your brush has a non-removable color cup, clean it with a swab. Clean an Aztek brush using its special cleaning tool/wrench.

E] Twist a corner of a paper towel into a point, dampen it with cleaner, and clean the inside of the nozzle. Never force anything, including pipe cleaners, through the nozzle. The tip on a double-action or hybrid brush is extremely fragile. If the nozzle and tip won't come clean, soak them in lacquer thinner or paint remover (depending on what type of paint is on it) until that paint softens or loosens. Then clean the nozzle using a piece of dampened toweling. Do not remove the tip from the nozzle.

F] Clean the needle by pulling it across a soft cloth dampened with the appropriate thinner/cleaner. Do not push it forward, and be careful—needles are sharp!

G] Reassemble the brush, then go to step 6 at left.

Airbrushing camouflage

Visualize it, name it, and sketch it—then you're ready to paint

BY SCOTT TRERROTOLA

Professional artist Scott Trerrotola airbrushes his WWII German armor paint schemes with the same creativity he uses in his work—and tells us how to approach the job.

German vehicles of World War II are my favorite subjects to model. The color schemes fascinate me, and the late war schemes offer modelers an especially wide range of colors and patterns. My research usually points my airbrush in a general direction, but copying color templates found in books is not always necessary. Since camouflage patterns were left to either the Panzer commander or the crew, there were no hard-and-fast rules to painting camouflage on German vehicles. The way I figure it, just let loose your creativity!

Ready? Before you start painting, start planning. Evaluate the shape of the vehicle, as its lines and contours can often dictate the patterns to choose. Sometimes I'll use colored pencils on photocopied line drawings to lay out a potential pattern.

The movement with which camouflage flows across a vehicle has a profound effect on the final result. Some vehicles look great with a diagonal pattern, while others look better with a random spray effect. Tiger-stripe patterns look good on just about anything, which brings me to an important point. Take notice of things in nature. Turtle shells, lizard-skin patterns, and even tree lines are all valid schemes for camouflage.

What's in a name? Naming your camouflage is a good way to keep pattern consistency before and during painting. For example, while airbrushing my Italeri Puma, I kept thinking "wild growing moss," and imagined the way moss grows on rocks and tree trunks. If I name the pattern and repeat it in my mind, I have less of a chance of spraying a pattern I don't intend. I know it sounds silly, but try it—it works!

Methods. My favorite painting tool is an airbrush, though spray cans too can be useful if the can is held far enough away from the surface of the model.

One technique is to use a light, dusting spray from a can over masks of pulled cotton that are secured with tack-putty or adhesive clay. This produces fine, dithered edges. Be sure to remove the cotton immediately after painting, or it will stick and ruin the effect. Hard lines can be masked easily with Silly Putty, which is easy to shape and won't pull up dry paint.

No matter how you choose to paint your armor, planning the pattern is the most important aspect of the overall appearance. All of the photoetched parts in the world won't substitute for a thoroughly planned, beautifully finished vehicle.

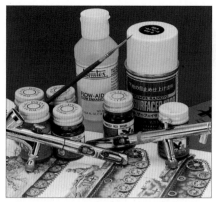

Scott starts with references, an airbrush, Polly Scale paints, Liquitex Flow Aid, and Gunze Sangyo primer. He then prepares his paint mixes: a base color, a shading color, and camouflage greens and browns.

For a model like this King Tiger, Scott first applies a base coat of light yellow. When this base coat is dry, he airbrushes a darker shade to highlight plates and panels.

Once the edges are highlighted, he "mists" the same color (by backing away the airbrush). Scott tries to retain the highlights, as the contrasts are very important.

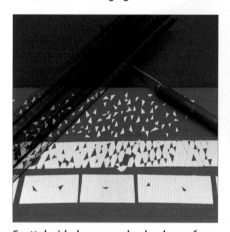

Scott decided on an ambush scheme for this particular Tamiya 1/35 scale King Tiger. He named it "ambush with triangular blowing leaves," and prepared by cutting up many small, triangular pieces of low-tack tape.

Next, he applies tape to predetermined areas of the tank. Keeping the camouflage's name in mind keeps the pattern consistent—here the leaves almost seem to swirl across the tank as if caught by a strong gust.

The second color of the camouflage is then airbrushed, while the low-tack tape holds to the model under the spray of fast-drying acrylic paint. Flow Aid keeps the edges smooth.

On this Tiger, he took the pattern one step further and applied masks for "blowing leaves" in both the sand yellow and the green. Normally, this step would involve covering all of the areas where brown and green have been painted. Instead, Scott masks in tight groups, keeping it simple.

The result is a unique and effective camouflage pattern. After a coat of clear gloss Scott applied decals, sealed them with clear flat, and began weathering. Dry transfers or stencil markings can be applied directly onto the paint with no clear overcoat.

After the hull and track assembly are complete, the tank's accessories and tools can be added. Look closely: Scott even painted grain onto the wooden handle of the shovel!

BY CHRIS APPOLDT AND TERRY THOMPSON / PHOTOS BY SCOTT TRERROTOLA

The answer is . . . ?

The multitude of schemes used by the Germans during WWII will allow you to indulge your artistic side.

For at least the last 300 years, almost certainly longer, soldiers have mimicked nature's camouflage schemes in hopes of concealing themselves from those hunting them. The armies of Germany, in their various forms, have been perhaps the foremost practitioners of the art of camouflage, first on their men, then on their machines.

During the 17th and 18th centuries, Germany's armies began enlisting Jägers (hunters), who were permitted to wear their traditional green clothing. By 1930, the post-World War I Reichsheer was issuing a camouflage combination tent-poncho (the Zeltbahn) to its troops, though the main uniform remained monochromatic. German AFVs wore camouflage even in World War I, in combinations of gray, green, and brown. From 1935 a new dark gray/dark brown pattern was standard, but a late 1939 order mandated an overall steel-gray color (RAL 7021 Gray, with a red iron-oxide primer coat underneath. The primer remained red oxide throughout the war.).

The Waffen-SS began using camouflaged uniforms early in the war, and shortly afterward the Wehrmacht began issuing camouflaged smocks (and eventually other garments) to its soldiers as well. German armor followed suit in 1943: an 18 February order mandated a base coat of RAL 7028 Dark Yellow with field-applied RAL 6003 Olive Green (sometimes called Dark Green) and RAL 8017 Red Brown camouflage. The green and brown paints were supplied as pastes, to be thinned before application with either gasoline (preferable, and used when plentiful) or water. The different thinners, different preferences of different units, and option of spray or brush application led to a wide and wild variety of patterns and color saturations on armor during this period. Gray vehicles at the front were not withdrawn for repainting, but were camouflaged with RAL 6003, 7028, and 8017 as needed. Zimmerit anti-magnetic-mine coating was used from early 1943 on tanks and assault guns.

As of 19 August 1944, however, these colors were factory-applied using spray guns to give soft edges in what has become known by modelers as the "ambush" pattern. Very shortly afterward (9 September 1944), the use of the Zimmerit coating was discontinued; it would be less common to find a factory ambush pattern on a Zimmerit-coated AFV.

As the situation in Germany deteriorated, adaptation and field improvisation became the order of the day, and AFV camouflage was no exception. As of 31 October 1944 the hulls were to be delivered in red oxide primer, with RAL 8017 Red Brown, RAL 6003 Green, and RAL 7028 Dark

Yellow camouflage patches to be applied by brush at the assembly plant. If the yellow was not available, RAL 7021 Gray (the early war base color) was an acceptable substitute camouflage color. It is possible that the change to this scheme was made earlier in the fall at some facilities, and photos indicate that the camouflage patches were applied occasionally with a spray gun.

This order remained in effect for only a month, however, as a 31 November 1944 order mandated that components arrive at the assembly plants with a base coat of RAL 6003 Green preapplied. There, camouflage of RAL 8017 Red Brown or RAL 7028 Dark Yellow was to be sprayed on (with sharp edges, though some sources suggest that both could be used). This scheme was to go into effect on 1 March 1945, but firms could switch as late as 30 May 1945, or earlier if possible.

After this order the situation in Germany became even more chaotic, and here is where the bulk of the questions remain. Apparently as of late winter 1944–45 some German AFVs were produced with base coats of Dark Yellow, sometimes with Red Brown and Green camouflage (the same colors as the ambush pattern, though likely applied in a different pattern), but sometimes not. While it is extremely unlikely, some may have had a base color of RAL 7021 Gray (!), with or without the Red Brown and Green patches (paint your late-war AFV model gray if you want debate the next time you enter a contest!). Add to this the fact that some units applied winter white washes, some may have applied camouflage in the field even late in the war, and repair depots occasionally had to repaint all or part of a vehicle, and the options are literally endless—and even controversial, when applied to a model. (And speaking of contentious topics, bet your buddies that they can't guess what the most common German AFV was in 1945. The answer isn't the King Tiger, Panther, or even the Panzer IV—it's the StuG III, and by a wide margin.)

Modelers of German AFVs, of course, love camouflage because it gives a model a unique paint finish and, ironically, makes it stand out in a crowd. However, these finishes also pose a challenge—not only in the masking and airbrushing department, but in research, where sometimes only black-and-white photographs exist for reference. The hunt is sometimes as much fun as the execution, though—especially when the final results can be so striking.

Straightforward masking and airbrushing techniques can produce stunning multicolor paint schemes on your cars, aircraft, and other models.

Painting complex graphics

Create award-winning finishes the Downie way

BY BOB DOWNIE

A custom-car model makes a great project for showing off your airbrushing talent. Creating cool graphics is relatively easy, and even though you can get similar effects in other ways, you will get the best results with your airbrush.

My choice for a car on which to do some easy, eye-catching graphics is Tamiya's 1/24 scale Toyota Celica (kit No. 24215) which features modern, new-edge styling. To me, the car looks very Ford-like, almost like Toyota's version of a pony car. So in the spirit of customization, I'll unashamedly borrow a basic paint scheme (with minor variations) and wheels from a Revell model, the Ford Mustang Super Stallion concept car (kit No. 2571).

I added a few custom details to the body for a more balanced look, namely air intakes below the headlights and some lower-body cladding, fashioned from half-round styrene strip. I also added a parts-box rear spoiler featuring scratchbuilt end plates. Here's how I went about finishing my Celica.

1 Here's the basic body with finished custom body treatments after it's been primed in white.

2 Fog some white primer from the sides onto the gray-molded chassis to get an authentic "factory" oversprayed appearance.

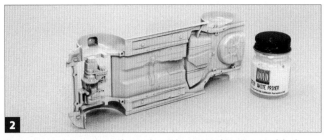

3 Gloss white is the base color for this model. It will allow subsequent colors to appear as bright and vivid as possible.

4 Bob uses Tamiya masking tape for clean color-separation lines and overall ease of use. A similar product is made by 3M.

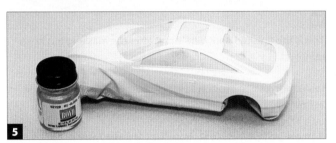

5 Thoroughly mask all areas you won't cover in yellow. Airbrush clear enamel onto the tape edges to prevent color bleed-through.

6 Airbrush the yellow base coat using Testor Model Master Bright Yellow enamel.

A primer coat. First, prepare the Celica body for primer. Clean it, remove mold lines, and add custom details. Mix Testor Model Master White Primer (No. 52719) with Testor Airbrush Thinner (No. 1799) until the mixture has the consistency of milk. Spray the entire model with a few light coats of primer.

Start with a fairly light coat. Build the beginning coats slowly. Hold the airbrush about 6" from the model, perpendicular to the surface. Use fluid arm strokes, moving the airbrush back and forth in a smooth, even manner over each surface of the model as the primer builds up. Start the flow before one end of the model, and continue beyond the other end.

The primer must flow smoothly. If it appears to be grainy, add a small amount of thinner. Test it on another surface, such as a scrap body, before applying it to your model. The primer should cover the body relatively quickly. Once the primer has completely covered the surface and is smooth, put the body aside to dry, **1**.

Next, apply primer to the chassis. Most unit-bodied chassis on cars are not completely painted. Usually, they are primed, and the body color is fogged onto the chassis' side surfaces from the outside inward. The center of the chassis often remains covered with just primer.

The kit chassis is molded in gray and looks enough like actual gray primer, so the white primer we add from the sides is for the effect of fogged-on body color.

Spray the chassis with white primer, holding the airbrush about 45 degrees below the bottom surface of the car. Cover the outside edges thoroughly, leaving the inner surfaces with a much thinner coat, **2**.

Each successive white paint coat added to the body during subsequent steps will be fogged onto the chassis. You don't have to be very careful with this part of the paint application, unless you are going for a full-custom effect on a car not intended for street driving.

A white base coat. Now give the car a base coat of white paint. Mix Testor Model Master High Gloss White (No. 52712) enamel with thinner to a milky consistency, and test the spray pattern to make sure the mixture flows well. Using the same technique as for applying the primer coat, spray the body while holding the airbrush perpendicular to the surface. Start with an overall light coat, and slowly build up successive coats until they are smooth and you have achieved complete coverage and color saturation, **3**. Once this is accomplished, set the model aside to dry. Gloss enamels usually take a week or so to dry thoroughly.

Make sure all the separate parts—such as mirrors and spoilers—are covered with the same number of coats as the body. And don't forget to clean the airbrush well once you're finished painting.

31

7

Mixing the pearl into the paint is easy – just add a pinch of pearl powder to clear enamel. Here's the clear pearl mixture ready for application. A small amount produces vivid results.

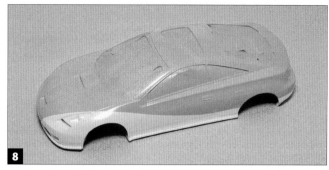

8

Here are the finished yellow areas after the masking has been removed.

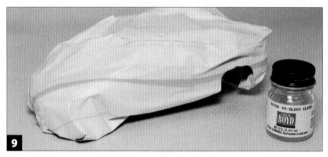

9

Mask off the body for the dark blue stripe. Don't forget to spray clear over the tape edges to prevent color bleed-through.

10

This is the finished dark blue stripe after the masking has been removed.

A yellow coat. Your next step is to add the yellow paint. First, mask all parts of the body that will remain white, **4**. I used Tamiya masking tape for the first layer of masking. It works well for masking custom paint schemes because it settles into body panel lines nicely, conforms well to curves, and is easily removed. Similar products, equally suitable for detailed masking, are also available from 3M in automotive paint stores.

Finish masking with regular masking tape and newspaper. Carefully seal all openings in the body, as paint overspray easily finds its way past small openings and is hard to remove.

When you have finished masking, seal the edges to prevent bleed-under of the color. Do this by using thinner to mix some Testor Model Master High Gloss Clearcoat enamel (No. 52720) to the consistency of milk and applying it to the edges of the masking material with your airbrush, **5**. Be careful to avoid spraying too much paint and causing a run.

Why go through this step? Because if there are tiny gaps in the masking, any paint that does bleed under is clear, and thus invisible. This trick is used by professionals and is good insurance.

When the clearcoat has dried thoroughly, you can paint the upper part of the body yellow. Mix the Testor Model Master Bright Yellow (No. 2717) to the proper consistency, and apply as in previous steps, slowly building it up to a smooth overall gloss. This will take several coats. Be patient!

Don't be tempted to prematurely wet-coat the paint, trying to build up the color intensity. Yellow requires more paint to achieve full-depth coverage than other colors. Make sure the paint covers the body thoroughly, and don't worry about making it completely glass-smooth on the first coats. Successive coats generally should go on a bit smoother and wetter, **6**. This technique takes practice.

Once the yellow is complete, let it dry, then clean your airbrush.

Leave the masking in place, and try to do the next step before the yellow paint has completely dried.

A pearl-yellow overcoat. Now the car is ready for a coat of pearl-yellow. Pearl powder is usually available in the paint section of art- and craft-supply stores, if you can't find it in your local hobby shop. Mix a small amount of pearl powder into thinned clear gloss enamel; it does not take a lot to achieve the desired effect, **7**.

Once it's mixed, airbrush the pearl directly over the yellow. Take care to apply it smoothly over the whole surface, and to apply the same number of coats to each panel. Use the same painting technique as for previous coats; however, the coat does not have to be super glossy, just smooth. The surface sheen can be a bit dull, as long as it is not grainy.

It takes only a few light coats to achieve the pearl effect. Once this has dried a bit (but not completely), carefully remove the outer masking from the body, **8**. Let the body dry, and thoroughly clean the airbrush.

A contrasting stripe. Next, you will add a dark, contrasting stripe to the body. As before, mask the body, using your own judgment as to the spacing and width of the stripe. After you've thoroughly masked the surface, add a clear sealer to the area to be painted, **9**.

For the stripe, I mixed Testor Model Master True Blue Pearl (No. 52706) and Testor Model Master Copenhagen Blue Metallic (No. 2703). Whatever color you use, thin this paint, then apply it in the same manner as previous coats. It builds up rapidly as you spray. Before the stripe is completely dry, remove the external masking materials, **10**.

The lower portion of the body is ready for pearly white paint. Add a pinch of pearl powder to some clear.

Match the interior color to the color of the carbon-fiber decals. I added custom decals to the seats, then sprayed the interior with Testor Dullcote for the proper flat sheen.

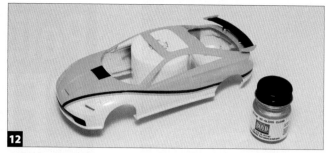

Add a few carbon-fiber decals, then coat the entire body with clear enamel.

Already a sleek car, the Celica acquires some pony-car pizzazz with a few custom details and a high-powered paint job.

Overcoats. You're ready to paint the lower portion of the body with a pearl-white overcoat. Mix a small amount of pearl powder into the thinned clear enamel, **11**. Again, mask all areas of the body that will not be covered in pearl white, leaving just the white base coat area exposed. Also, have another bottle of clear enamel mixed with thinner ready (to clear-coat the entire body after you have applied the pearl white).

Don't worry about a very slight tint to the clear enamel; it rarely is visible on a finished model, since the coats are so thin. Also, you may notice that some bottles of clear enamel are more transparent than others. Always test a new brand out over your base coats first, to be sure it won't cause the paint underneath to crack or "lift."

Apply the pearl white as in previous steps, then remove the masking and add several coats of clear enamel to the body. Again, begin slowly, making successive coats wetter. You must apply a good coat of clear without obliterating engraved detail. You need just enough so you can buff only clear enamel when you're polishing the model, **12**. After the clear has dried, you can add other paint and decal details to the body.

The interior. Mix the interior color to match the color of carbon-fiber decals on the exterior. I painted the interior a flat dark brown mixed with black.

I added Scale Motorsport Leopard Pattern upholstery decals (No. 1974) for extra detail. To make the surface gloss of these decals match the finish of the flat interior colors, tone them down. Airbrush a mixture of Testor Dullcote (No. 1160) clear lacquer over the decals and the rest of the interior, **13**. This creates the convincing appearance of automotive upholstery; without the Dullcote, the decals would be too glossy.

Use your imagination. At this point, you're on your own! Polish the body and add all assembly and finishing details to the model. The finished model will look sharp, and the masking and painting techniques you've acquired can be used for any custom or street-rod project.

As you gain experience, your imagination is the only limiting factor. You can airbrush flames, scallops, or multicolored effects such as murals or the patterns commonly seen on lowriders or street rods. Let your imagination run wild, use the proper tools and techniques, and your models will reflect your own personal designs.

BOB'S TOP FIVE TIPS

1] Simulate fogged-on body color on your chassis by thoroughly applying body paint to the chassis' edges while holding the airbrush about 45 degrees below the chassis' surface.

2] Make sure all the separate parts—such as mirrors and spoilers—are covered with the same number of coats of paint as the body.

3] When you finish masking, airbrush a coat of thinned gloss clear over the edges of the masking material. If there are gaps in the masking, any paint that bleeds under will be clear, and thus invisible.

4] Don't be tempted to prematurely wet-coat the paint. Start with light coats, which may be a bit grainy. Then build up to a smooth finish with successive coats.

5] Don't worry if there's a slight tint to your clear gloss when it's still in the bottle; your coats of clear will be so thin that the tint will rarely—if ever—be noticeable on your finished models.

The airbrush is nifty, but other magical tools exist to help you finish models. Read on to discover polish, frisket, and foil, and make your models look even better.

Polished to PERFECTION

Achieving a high-gloss, mirror-like finish on your models isn't as hard as it looks; in fact, it's as easy as 1-2-3—or maybe 4000-6000-8000.

Bring out the shine in your model's finish

BY PAT COVERT / PHOTOS BY THE AUTHOR

Getting a mirror-like, high-gloss finish on a model these days is easier than ever before, due mainly to the advent of the polishing kit. These kits come in a variety of configurations, or you can customize your own—but they all use the same method for polishing out a gloss surface.

Polishing, or "rubbing out," a gloss finish is essentially a four-part process. First, a coarse grit levels out any texture found on the surface of the paint. Second, a succession of finer grits continuously remove scratches in the surface until none are left. Third, a polish removes any haze and minute scratches left by the sanding process. Finally, a wax or protectant is employed to bring the paint up to full luster.

Polish your nerve. If you've never polished out a paint job before, you probably find the thought of sanding on such a small, fragile surface a bit scary. Don't worry. The grits in a polishing kit are relatively fine to begin with, and the finest grits are virtually indiscernible to the touch from one to the next. Like all modeling processes, practice is the key—so jump in and get your feet wet.

Our test model is an AMT/Ertl Plymouth Street Fury with all of the trim removed for a clean, oh-so-smooth look. The body is painted in Tamiya Italian Red (TS8) aerosol lacquer. The paint job is already very slick right out of the can, but virtually any paint is going to impart some level of texture—the Fury definitely had a random texture that could be improved. Follow along as we polish our little Plymouth's paint job to perfection!

Leveling the paint. Before you pick up the first sanding pad, it is important to make sure you have adequate paint depth or you'll sand through to the primer and plastic. Typically, an enamel paint job should have four to five wet coats of paint applied to the surface. A lacquer paint job should have more, because lacquer is applied in much thinner coats. If you are at all in doubt about the depth, try your first polishing job on a scrap piece of plastic and give the process a run-through before working on the model.

Sanding mediums come in three basic forms: cloths, pads, and sheets, **1**. Both cloths and pads have a fabric backing that allows the surface of the medium to conform to the contours, though sanding sheets have a clear acetate backing that tends to make them stiffer. This makes them harder to use during the sanding process. I much prefer the fabric-backed cloths and pads, **2**. Of the cloth sanding grits, my preference is the sanding pads. These 2" x 2" pads have a foam core sandwiched between two layers of sanding medium, **3**. I find them much easier to manipulate than the sanding cloths, which are used in conjunction with a foam block. The downside to using the pads is wet sanding—I have had the grit cloth separate from the foam core with repeated wet use.

Both cloths and pads work fine, however, and they are equally effective. I suggest you try both to see which fits

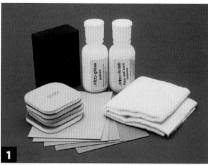

1. Polishing cloths and pads are the workhorses of any polishing kit and can produce brilliant finishes. You'll need polish, some soft flannel cloth, and a sanding block to use with the cloth.

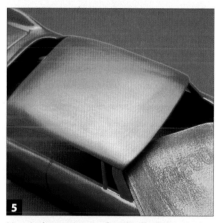

3. The Tamiya Italian Red lacquer went down beautifully, but most paints impart some texture. Use polishing pads to level out the paint for a super-slick finish.

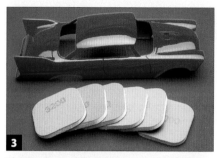

5. Here's the entire roof with all of the texture removed. No shine remains on the surface, indicating that the paint is leveled.

your fancy. Micro-Mark offers a choice of cloths or pads. Other companies offer sets of cloths and pads separately.

Wet or dry? There has always been a question when using a polishing kit of whether to wet-sand (in wet sanding, constantly wet the medium with water to flush particles from the sandpaper grit,

2. The cloths are numbered by grit on the back side. The higher the number, the finer the grit. Most kits have coarser grits than 3200 included, but they're generally too coarse for rubbing out a finish.

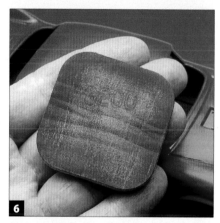

4. Half of the roof has been sanded smooth (left half) with the 3200-grit while the other half remains untouched by the pad. The finer grits will bring back the luster.

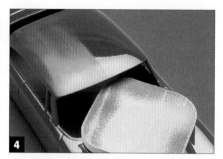

6. As you can see, the 3200-grit pad removes a lot of paint. Notice also the creases in the pad where it was folded in order to get into tight spots.

keeping it consistently abrasive) or to dry-sand. It's easier to gauge your progress when dry sanding, and I recommend that beginners use this technique initially. By doing so, you'll get a better feel for exactly what the sanding mediums are actually doing during the process. I prefer to dry-sand with the first grit just to make sure my surface has been completely leveled.

7

The 3200-grit pad has done its work. I stayed away from the high spots, particularly on the fins, because there was very little texture in these areas and I didn't want to cut through to the primer below.

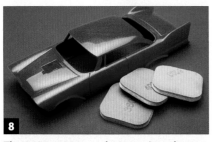

8

The 3600-, 4000-, and 6000-grit pads are used in succession to remove scratches in the surface. Wet-sanding with these pads keeps the grits clean. At this point you can see the luster returning to the paint.

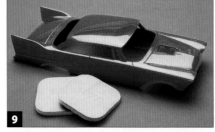

9

What a difference the 8000-and 12000-grit pads make! By the time you reach this stage the paint will be up to a high luster with only a slight haze remaining on the surface. The polish will take care of that.

10

A two-step system that works well is a plastic polish called Novus, which comes in formulas #1 and #2. The Novus #2 is used to polish out the surface, while the #1 is used as a glossing agent and protectant.

11

Polish is applied in circular strokes, much as you would shine your shoes. Always use a soft cloth such as flannel for polishing. A coarse fabric can actually add scratches to the surface.

From there, I wet-sand—it's quicker because the grits stay cleaner as you work. Wet-sanding also extends the life of the cloth because it washes away much of the residue that tends to clog up the grit. It's strictly a matter of personal preference and has no noticeable impact on the quality of the finished surface.

The first sanding grit is the most critical one you'll use; its purpose is to level out the entire painted surface. Successively finer grits—one by one—are used to remove scratches from the painted surface. In most instances you will start with the 3200-grit, which works well for removing a typical amount of texture. If you have a particularly slick paint job to begin with, you may wish to start with the 3600-grit.

Begin by sanding the area with back-and-forth strokes—never sand in circles! The sanding stroke will vary in width depending on how much surface area you have to work with. The broader the panel, the wider the stroke, **4**. With these fine grits you can reverse direction, but don't crosshatch if you can help it. As you begin sanding, you will note that a dull texture will appear on the high spots of the paint while the low areas remain glossy. Go slowly at all times and inspect your progress as you go, **5**. Keep sanding until all the gloss in the low spots has been removed. Be especially careful sanding around sharp edges and high spots—the paint is thinner here, so it's much easier to cut through to the primer or plastic below. On the plus side, paint is generally smoother around these areas, so you can just sand close to them. When necessary, fold the pad or cloth (without the sanding block) or use just a corner of the sanding medium to get into the tight spots, **6**.

The goal is to sand the entire surface (with the exception of the previously mentioned high spots and edges) until it is consistently dull all over, **7**. This indicates that the paint has been leveled. Repeat this process on each panel until all surface texture has been removed.

Removing scratches. The purpose of the remaining cloths or pads is to remove all minute scratches from the finish. This is done by using successively finer grits to sand the surface until it's scratch-free. The sanding process continues as you move up through the numerical succession of sanding cloths (the higher the number, the finer the grit). You won't need to spend as much time using these grits as you did sanding with the first one.

The 3600-grit cloth will remove any scratches left by the coarser 3200-grit cloth. After you have sanded the entire body using the 3600-grit cloth, you'll do the entire process again using the 4000-grit cloth. From 4000 you will move up to 6000, then 8000, and finally 12000. Never skip a grit in the sanding process—you'll end up with scratches that can only be removed by going back and re-sanding with the previous grits. Watch carefully as you go from one grit to the next, and you'll notice the scratches getting finer and finer along the way. This is a sure sign you're on the right track, **8**.

You will start seeing the gloss return to the paint by the time you have finished sanding with the 6000-grit sanding cloth. The 8000 and 12000-grit cloths restore virtually all of the glossy shine to the surface and leave only a haze that must be polished out. At this point you will begin to appreciate the benefits of the polishing kit, **9**.

Polishing. The purpose of polish is to remove any haze and extremely fine scratches left by the final sanding. There are a myriad of polishes to choose from, some that are supplied in polishing kits and others that are available separately. The polish is meant to remove any scratches left by the sanding grit, and the anti-haze and swirl brings a high gloss to the surface, **10**.

Polishing paint is very much like shining your shoes. Stick your finger into a soft flannel cloth, add a little polish to the tip of your finger, and go to town, **11**. Unlike the sanding procedure, polishing is done using circular strokes. Polish should be rubbed into the surface of the paint using medium pressure. Just as when you were sanding, care should be taken not to rub too hard around the sharp edges of parts where paint tends to be thinner. Once you have fully polished out an area, switch to a clean area of the cloth and buff away any excess polish. This final buffing should reveal a blazing shine, **12**. Note: always test products not specifically made for scale automotive finishes on painted scrap plastic. Certain polishes may

12 Look at those reflections! The polish imparts a blazing shine to the finish. Don't be alarmed that the cloth picks up paint residue. It's part of the process.

13 A sealant or protectant, in this case Novus #1, adds even more gloss—plus a certain amount of protection from handling and oxidation.

Here's the Plymouth Street Fury ready for show. Go the extra mile on your next project by polishing out your paint—it's the crowning touch to any gloss finish!

be too harsh for use on softer paints such as hobby enamels.

An ounce of protection. A gloss protectant will add more shine to your model and will help safeguard the finish as well. If your polishing kit did not come supplied with a protectant, purchase one. Protectants usually fall into two categories: wax-based and silicone-based. The Last Detail Final Treatment Wax is a carnuba-based wax that works well for both adding gloss and protection. Novus #1 is a silicone-based protectant that adds a glass-like finish to the surface, **13**.

Protectants, like polishes, are applied with a flannel cloth, and you'll use the same circular motion when applying them. I recommend using a separate cloth rather than the one used for applying polish to eliminate the possibility of contamination between the two. I keep an abundance of flannel on hand so I can use a clean piece for each application—it's inexpensive and readily available at your local fabric store.

Once applied, a protectant will give the painted surface a super-high shine and help protect the model when handled, as well as from extraneous damage such as oxidation. These products do indeed vary in consistency and chemical make-up, so practice a bit with them.

Approved narcissism. Okay, so I need to add an additional step—what good is applying a great finish to a model if you can't sit back and enjoy it? Once you've got your model assembled, spend a little quiet time with it. I usually set this time aside on a Friday night at home. First, I'll put on one of my favorite CDs, one that reflects the mood of the model I've just completed; rock and roll for a '32 Deuce, hard rock for a street machine, jazz for a sports car, or . . . well, you got the picture. I set the model on the coffee table in front of me and reflect on the build. All of this is much more pleasurable when you've got a killer finish, so get out that polishing kit and add some brilliance to your project.

Foiled
LIGHTNING

How to finish your plane with aluminum foil

BY BUCKY SHEFTALL / PHOTOS BY THE AUTHOR

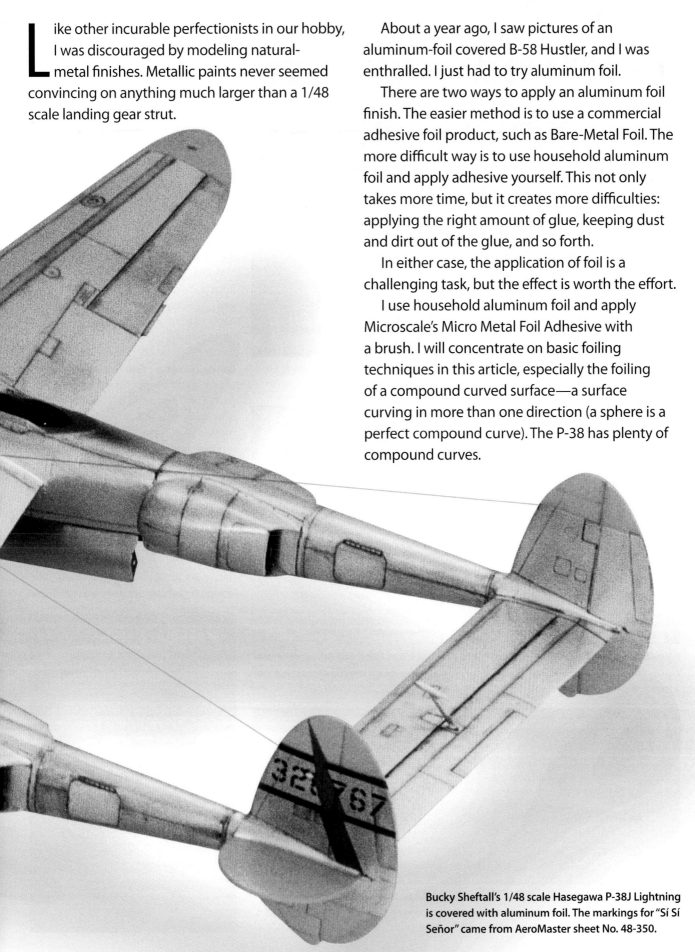

Like other incurable perfectionists in our hobby, I was discouraged by modeling natural-metal finishes. Metallic paints never seemed convincing on anything much larger than a 1/48 scale landing gear strut.

About a year ago, I saw pictures of an aluminum-foil covered B-58 Hustler, and I was enthralled. I just had to try aluminum foil.

There are two ways to apply an aluminum foil finish. The easier method is to use a commercial adhesive foil product, such as Bare-Metal Foil. The more difficult way is to use household aluminum foil and apply adhesive yourself. This not only takes more time, but it creates more difficulties: applying the right amount of glue, keeping dust and dirt out of the glue, and so forth.

In either case, the application of foil is a challenging task, but the effect is worth the effort.

I use household aluminum foil and apply Microscale's Micro Metal Foil Adhesive with a brush. I will concentrate on basic foiling techniques in this article, especially the foiling of a compound curved surface—a surface curving in more than one direction (a sphere is a perfect compound curve). The P-38 has plenty of compound curves.

Bucky Sheftall's 1/48 scale Hasegawa P-38J Lightning is covered with aluminum foil. The markings for "Sí Sí Señor" came from AeroMaster sheet No. 48-350.

Nothing looks more like aluminum than aluminum. Adhesive-backed aluminum foil is available in many hobby shops, or you can add adhesive to household foil.

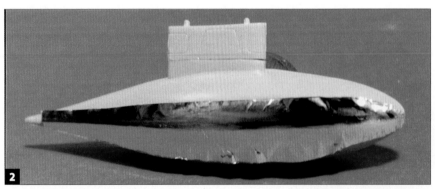

1

If you aren't using Bare-Metal Foil, you'll need to brush Micro Metal Foil Adhesive on the matte side of household aluminum foil. The folded-over edge on the foil sheet serves as a handle.

2

Applying foil to compound curves, such as those of this P-38 drop tank, is the most difficult part of the process. Here's how to start: Cut a thin strip of foil and lightly press it onto the tank along the middle.

Getting around it. The harsh reality of foiling is that you are trying to apply a two-dimensional material to a three-dimensional object. Household foil has almost no stretchiness, and can be torn or wrinkled if forced around a sharp compound curve. Bare-Metal Foil stretches better over curves.

While it is desirable to minimize joints by using large pieces of foil on large, flat areas, such as wings or control surfaces, small curved items should be covered in small pieces to avoid wrinkles.

For my example, I'm going to foil over the teardrop-shaped P-38 150-gallon fuel tank first. There are plenty of curves here: it has a round cross-section, a blunt nose, and a radically tapered tail. Sweat beads begin to form on my brow just looking at the drop tank!

Ready . . . set . . . foil! The first step is to sand away all imperfections from the parts. Foil is not going to cover seams or irregularities—it's only going to make them look worse!

Once you have smoothed the item, wash it with soapy water so oils don't reduce adhesion of the foil. Remove any lint or sanding dust anywhere that could be conspicuously trapped by the foil.

If you are using Bare-Metal Foil, you can skip this next step. When using household foil, cut a suitably sized piece and lay it on a clean work surface with the foil's matte side facing up. The fluid adhesive spreads better

MATERIALS LIST

- either Bare-Metal Foil (regular "chrome" is best) or the thinnest aluminum foil you can find
- Microscale Metal Foil Adhesive
- a couple of flat artist's brushes, 1.5cm (about ½") wide
- glass, Plexiglas, or coated, lint-free cardboard work surface
- scissors
- sharp hobby knife blades or razor blades
- fine steel wool (0000)
- cotton swabs
- round toothpicks
- rubbing alcohol
- facial tissues

on the matte side. Don't worry about the overly shiny side of the foil; you'll be taking care of that later. Fold ¼" of one end over on itself to serve as a handle.

Apply Micro Metal Foil Adhesive with a flat brush. Keep brush strokes roughly parallel, pushing away from the handle to spread the liquid in a thin, even layer, **1**. Be careful not to let any dust get on the foil, especially while the adhesive is drying. When the milky liquid dries to an even, Scotch-tape-like clear matte appearance, the pressure-activated adhesive is ready, and the foil can be applied to the model.

One piece at a time. Cut a strip of foil slightly longer than the tank and a width (varying with the shape of the tank) maybe one-sixth of the circumference. The fraction is not important, just try to keep the edges straight along the axis of the tank. Lightly press the strip onto the tank at the midpoint, and adjust the position, **2**. As you can see in the photo, wrinkles are already evident and will likely get worse as you work the foil down.

Burnish the strip onto the tank with a cotton swab, **3**. Increasing the pressure will activate the adhesive. The wrinkles on my tank weren't as bad as I thought they would be, and they were easy to rub out with toothpicks and steel wool.

Lightly sand the edges of the strip with 1000-grit sandpaper or an ultra-fine sanding stick. Sand perpendicular to the edge and push away from the edge of the foil strip. This will feather the edge, reducing the "cliff" and allowing the overlap of the next foil segment to become nearly invisible.

Continue laying strips, **4**, until the entire tank is covered, **5**. Thin (⅛"-wide) strips can be burnished over the prominent raised fuel tank seams.

Reducing the shine. A rubdown (front to back) with 0000 steel wool gives a "grain" or patina to the too-shiny foil and makes it look more like real aircraft skin. The steel wool also helps obscure the fine edges of the foil segments, **6**.

After the tank and its pylon are completely foiled, wash it with warm soapy water to remove finger oils (which can oxidize on the foil and leave dark gray fingerprints) and remove the grains of aluminum dust generated by the sandpaper and steel wool. It is essential

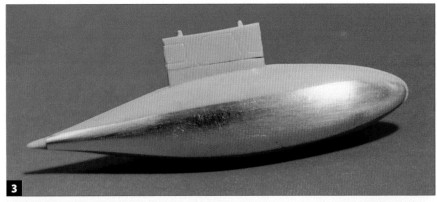

3

Burnish the strip onto the part with a cotton swab, then go over the edges with an ultra-fine sanding stick.

4

The next piece of foil overlaps the first and then is burnished in place.

5

Lightly sanding the edges of the foil helps the next piece hide the overlap.

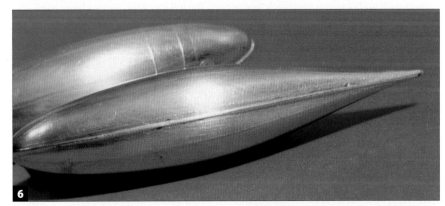

6

Once the covered tank is scoured with 0000 steel wool, the seams between the pieces of foil practically disappear.

7

The rear of the Lightning's central pod is another curved area. The foil is lightly tacked in place.

8

Burnishing begins with a cotton swab . . .

9

. . . and ends with a round toothpick that pushes the foil into and over surface detail.

10

With the foil burnished in place, the edges can be trimmed with a sharp blade.

to remove this dust before the next step. That's the basic technique for foiling, which is repeated over and over with slight variations according to the shapes of the parts, **7** through **10**. Larger or flatter parts are easier to cover.

Tips for better foiling. When foiling a wing or stabilizer, wrap the top-surface foil over the leading edge, **11**, so the seam is on the under-surface where it is less conspicuous, **12**. Burnish foil over raised or recessed panel lines, and use those lines as trim points between pieces of foil. Use only a sharp blade to cut the foil along the panel lines. The adjacent piece of foil overlaps the panel line and should be trimmed in the same manner.

To cover small intake scoops such as the one on the side of the P-38 engine cowl, make a slit along the leading edge of the scoop before burnishing the foil. This will allow the foil to conform. Cover any "bald spots" with little "toupee strips" of foil, then burnish and polish with steel wool as usual, **13**.

If you find small unfoiled spots, cover them with small patches of foil, or touch up with slightly thinned aluminum paint after the model is finished.

Bursting bubbles. If you find an air bubble under the foil, slit it with a sharp

BARE-METAL FOIL

If you don't want the hassle of applying adhesive to foil, you can obtain ultra-thin aluminum foil with a pressure-sensitive adhesive already on it. Bare-Metal Foil was one of the original foils for modelers, developed in the early 1970s. Other brands of self-stick foils have come and gone, but Bare-Metal Foil is still around.

Bare-Metal Foil is an aluminum alloy that has more malleability than standard household foil, and it's thinner, too. It comes in 6" x 12" sheets, mounted on a waxy paper. You remove it by scoring through the foil with a sharp blade, peeling the foil from the paper with tweezers, and transferring it to the model.

In addition to the regular chrome finish, BMF is also available in ultra-bright chrome, matte aluminum, black-chrome, real copper, and gold-colored versions.

blade, then burnish it with a toothpick. Be careful not to snag the edge of the slit with the toothpick, which would cause the foil to rip. Rub steel wool over the area, and the bubble and slit will disappear.

It's usually a good idea to foil sub-assemblies before attaching them to the model. Keep in mind, though, that the areas to be bonded must be free of foil. You can touch up the glue joints with bits of foil after final assembly.

Sealing the foil. After you "grain" the foil with steel wool, wipe away excess adhesive with a tissue dampened in rubbing alcohol. Next, wash the entire model with warm, soapy water, wipe away excess water, and let the model air-dry.

Apply several coats of Future acrylic floor polish with a flat, carefully cleaned brush or an airbrush. Future seals the foil, protects it from oxidation, and forms a primer coat that is needed under any additional painting or weathering. (Enamels, artist's oils, lacquers, or acrylic paints don't adhere well to bare foil.) Future also adds to the luster of the metal and forms a perfect surface for applying decals.

Try it, you'll like it! To me, foil is the most realistic natural-metal finish. Well, outside of scratchbuilding from sheets of aluminum, that is.

11 Large, flat areas are a little easier to foil. Here a strip has been gently laid onto the horizontal stabilizer. Excess foil will wrap around at the leading edge.

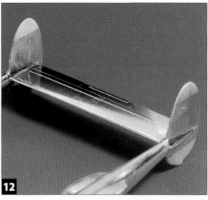

12 Now the foil has been burnished down, but it has yet to be scoured with steel wool.

13 Foiling over small scoops can be done with small strips of foil. Slicing through the foil at scoop openings allows the foil to work around the holes.

Bucky's foil-finished fighter looks like it is made of aluminum. But the metal is only skin deep.

You don't have to paint hot rod flames to use this handy frisket paper technique. Professional illustrator Tim Phelps shows how you can create reusable painting masks.

Eternal FLAMES

Create reusable frisket masks for custom paint jobs

BY TIM PHELPS / PHOTOS BY JIM DURHAM

When I held my first 1/64 scale car—a Jaguar XKE—at the age of seven, I was hooked. Eventually I combined that love with a fondness for hot rod culture and modeling. More recently, I've customized car models with airbrushing, along with hand-painting techniques I've used for five years.

With a variety of die-cast metal cars on the market, I can live the customizer's dream and create personal cruisers in a multitude of colors with hot licks and streaking flames—and you can, too. Though I choose to customize in 1/64 scale, the steps presented here can easily apply to models in any scale—just make sure the base coat has already cured. Now, flame on!

1

To prepare a painting mask, start by sketching your flame design on tracing paper. Then test-fit it to make sure the flames are where you want them.

2

Put a fresh blade on your hobby knife before cutting the frisket—any nicks or glue drops will snag the delicate film.

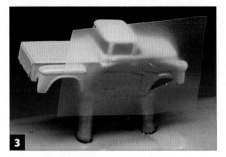

3

For the basic flame technique, press the frisket paper firmly in place, then spray the main color. After the paint is completely dry, you can outline the flames.

4

On this '41 Willys, Tim sprayed orange at the tail end and lime at the hood end. To achieve a gradual fade, spray lighter colors first, then the darker colors.

Wild fire. Begin by sketching flames on tracing paper. Keep the shape of the side panel in mind—including the roofline, the windows, and the wheel wells—and doodle different flame configurations. Observe the body, following its lines and imagining a flame style that will fit your "canvas."

Tracing paper allows you to sketch your design, cut it up, and paste it up into different configurations. For symmetrical flames, draw half of your spread of flames on tracing paper and fold the drawing at the flame's edge, **1**. Then just turn the paper over, retrace the other side, and unfold it. Asymmetry may be just fine, too—you can see only one side of the car at a time.

Drape the final sketch over the body panel, roof, fenders, and hood for a placement check. Tracing paper is thin enough to press into the nooks of the fenders if necessary. Once you have finalized your flame layout, cut a piece of frisket film (available from art-supply stores) to size, remove it from its carrier sheet, and place it tacky-side-down over the sketch.

Making the mask. With a sharp No. 11 blade in your hobby knife, carefully cut out the flames. Try to cut into the points and

corners, not out of them, to reduce the risk of tearing or stretching the film, **2**. The knife handle should rest comfortably in your hand; don't grip it too hard. The blade should glide over your sketch while you cut the film so you make smooth curves.

Carefully peel the film from the sketch. Position the opening onto the area of the car to be airbrushed and gently press out any air bubbles with your fingers. Use low-tack masking tape to cover and protect the portions of the car body that won't be painted.

By the way, all these parts are reusable. Repair blade cuts on your sketch by placing clear adhesive tape over the drawing. You can use the mask once or twice more before it loses its stickiness. Save the cut-out flames, too—they can be used later on other cool customs.

Spraying the paint. Use an airbrush with a fine spray. I use a Paasche AB to produce medical and scientific illustrations, and its fine action even allows me to write my name with it. Olympus and Iwata are two other good brands to consider. Visit an art-supply store and try one out. Talk to your friends, too, and find out what they recommend.

The paint (I use Testor and Model Master enamels, but acrylics work fine, too) should be thinned but not too watery—try for the consistency of milk. Using a small brush, dip into your paint and fill the airbrush cup (but not to overflowing). You're now ready to spray your base flame color into the opening of the film mask, **3**.

To minimize an edge on the flame, keep your coats thin and allow them to dry between applications. Try not to overspray in any one area. By working back and forth, you can apply a thin and even base coat over the entire flame area. Turn the car to ensure proper angles for paint coverage.

After a brief drying time, carefully remove the mask and reveal the flames, **4**. Start peeling at the flame tips to avoid pulling up paint or stretching the mask. Replace the used mask on its original carrier sheet.

Getting singed? To correct any slips of the brush or overspray from the airbrushing, use Oops brand latex paint remover to clean your flames. (Mineral spirits will also work.) Dip a small brush into the liquid and dab it once on a rag. A small amount of the liquid will remain on the brush, and you can brush along the area to be corrected, **5**. The

45

paint should lift right off! After one or two swipes of the brush, just dip, dab, and brush again. Don't let the fluid form a bead on the end of your brush—it can smear the flame.

Keep in mind that the body color plays a major part in the visual impact of your final flames or graphics, **6**. To produce colored flames on a white-bodied car, use a frisket mask with the flame section removed. Airbrush your flames, then remove the mask and clean up your flame edges. For white flames on a colored car, use the flame section of the frisket as the mask, then airbrush the rest of the car.

To add another dimension to your flames, try outlining them. For this close-up work, I recommend wearing an Optivisor magnifier. With the car body on the paint stand, select a small (6/0) sable liner brush and apply paint with a small bead on the brush tip. Slowly pull the paint along the outline of the flame,

7. Turn the body of the car on its stand as needed to find the best angle from which to paint. If you make mistakes, just keep on painting. You can correct mistakes later with the interior flame color, the exterior body color, or with paint remover.

Advanced techniques. You can also paint flames without using a mask, as I did with these vintage race cars, **8**. Start by holding the car in your hand. Stroke the flames from their points forward on the car, turning your imagination loose as you follow the curve of the car body. Angle the tip of the brush to shape the line precisely. Next, add an interior color—the first color will serve as the outline. This method allows for exact shaping and detailing of each flame—outside by the body color, and inside by the interior flame color.

By outlining along the entire flame in a lighter or darker color, you can achieve a pinstriping effect. The striping gives definition to your design, **9**. Give it depth by highlighting with a light color on the top or bottom of the flame only. Add a "drop shadow" with a darker shade of the body color along the underside or bottom of the flame length, giving the illusion of depth. Be inventive: consider the attitude of your custom cruiser and flame accordingly.

For inspiration, take a glance at past and present hot rod and custom magazines and let your imagination wander. Discover the rich history of flame painting, and re-create the various styles and combinations that have evolved over the last 60 years. The great thing about hot rods and customs is that almost any color scheme is acceptable. Attitude is everything—the car's and yours—so have some fun!

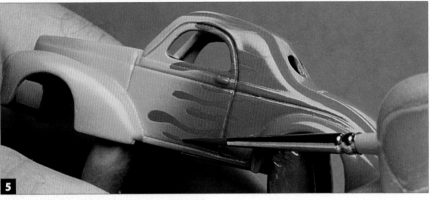

5

With a small brush and a bit of latex paint remover, you should be able to clean up any problems along the edges of the flames.

6

These Merc "tail draggers" show that you can use both parts of the frisket mask, depending on which area of the car you'll paint.

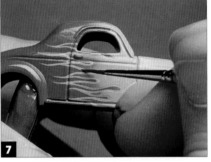

7

To give your flames a finished look, outline them in a contrasting color with a small sable brush. Work from the point of the flame forward, and take your time.

8

These three vintage racers were hand-painted, not airbrushed. To use this technique, outline the flame first, then fill it in later.

9

Creative outlining can help you add depth to the model. The color choice can make a big difference in the final look.

Armor
WHITEWASH

Create convincing winter camouflage with artist's pastels

BY JOHN ROBINSON / PHOTOS BY THE AUTHOR

BEFORE

John Robinson created authentic winter camouflage on this Soviet JS-2 tank using his easy whitewash technique.

AFTER

For armored vehicles, survival often depends on blending into the surrounding landscape. During World War II, when the harsh European winter blanketed the landscape with snow, spring and summer camouflage was useless—even dangerous—against the white backdrop. To make their vehicles less vulnerable, armies adopted temporary whitewash winter camouflage schemes. I've developed an easy method for re-creating the scruffy look of winter-time camouflage. It uses common materials and simple techniques and can be modified easily to suit individual needs and preferences.

Before you begin, think about the situations where this camouflage was applied. Field conditions were not ideal, and supplies were not plentiful. Period photographs indicate that vehicles were haphazardly whitewashed with whatever was available. Such field-applied camouflage was often poor to start with and deteriorated quickly in the harsh weather.

6

Weathering

Once the finish is on, you can enhance it with washes, dry-brushing, and pastel chalks. Add a little rust here and there, and transform your models into realistic miniature masterpieces.

Scrape off a small pile of pastel powder with your hobby knife. A teaspoonful should be enough to do the job for most models.

Add water one drop at a time and mix to the consistency of hobby paint.

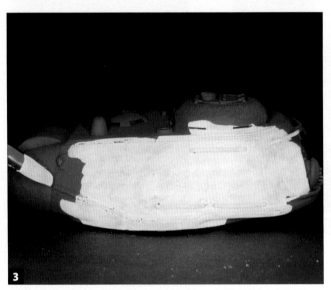

Apply the whitewash with a soft, wide brush. There's no need to fuss about neatness—brush marks actually add realism.

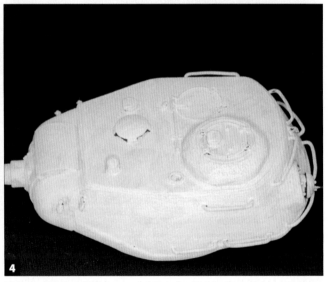

The model should be covered, but the finish doesn't have to be perfectly even.

Preparations. Needed materials are easy to find and use: white artist's pastel chalk, water, an eyedropper, a mixing cup, hobby knife or scalpel, paintbrushes, a toothbrush or other stiff-bristled brush, a wire brush (optional), cotton swabs, and flat clearcoat. Make sure you get dry pastels; the waxy, oil-based variety will not work.

Of course, you'll also need a model. The "before" photo on page 47 shows my 1/35 scale Dragon Soviet JS-2 tank prepped for the whitewash. The green base color has cured, and the markings have been sealed with flat clearcoat.

Your model's tools and other details may be painted either before or after the whitewash is applied. A clear matte finish will help the whitewash adhere, but it's not required.

Gently scrape the pastel stick with your hobby knife to make a pile of powder in the mixing cup, **1**. A teaspoonful of powder should be enough for most models. It's best to scrape off a little more powder than you think you'll need.

Add water to the pastel in the mixing cup one drop at a time, stirring after each drop, **2**. Aim for a consistency similar to hobby paint—only a few drops of water are necessary. A mixture that is too thin will not cover well; one that's too thick will clump and look unrealistic.

Applying the whitewash. Paint the model with the pastel mixture using a soft, wide paintbrush, **3**. Even strokes are best, but neatness is not necessary or even desirable, **4**; in real life, crews didn't cover every nook and cranny. Visible brush marks actually add realism, as does paint over the markings.

Let the whitewash dry before the next step. Use a hair dryer to speed the drying.

Simulating wear. Using a clean, dry paintbrush of medium stiffness, brush the whitewash back and forth with short strokes, **5**. This rubs off some pastel and creates the desired scruffy look.

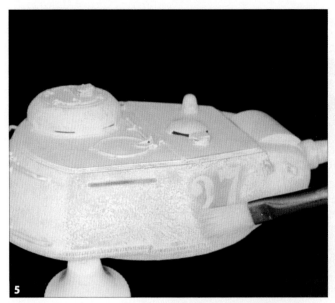

After the whitewash has dried, scrape it off with a stiff brush using short back-and-forth strokes.

John sprayed earth brown on the suspension, tracks, and other areas that would get dirty during operation.

The crevices and low spots should remain white, while heavy wear areas such as edges, handles, and crew traffic paths should show the underlying color. This is the time to even out pastel clumps and brush marks.

Use different-size brushes to get varied results. Smaller ones will reach tight spots. Stiff-bristle brushes will remove the whitewash quickly; soft-bristle ones will impart subtler wear.

Scratch the whitewash with a wire brush for extra effect. A cotton swab barely moistened with water will remove the whitewash and uncover the markings hidden when the whitewash was applied. You can use a wet paintbrush to remove parts of the whitewash and create streaks.

If you take off too much whitewash, just apply another coat and try again. If you make a major mistake, wash the model in water and start over. Take advantage of this technique's flexibility and control to achieve the desired appearance.

Sealing the whitewash. Once you have the whitewash the way you want, seal it to make it permanent and prevent damage when you weather it.

Airbrush a thin coat of clear flat, such as Testor's Model Master Acryl. This diminishes the whitewash effect, but that's normal. Apply more whitewash if necessary once the clear finish is dry, then spray on more clearcoat. Repeat the steps until you're satisfied with the result.

Weathering. You can enhance the model's appearance by dry-brushing with the base color, or an earth color for a dirtier look. Use a wide, flat paintbrush that has been wiped on a rag to remove all but slight traces of pigment. Lightly brush over the model's surface; after a few passes, the color will appear on surface textures. With this approach, you can add suggestions of color only where needed.

Finishing touches. Frozen earth and melting snow splash around the tracks and coat a vehicle's running gear, **6**. Simulate

Worn whitewash camouflage adds a final, compelling touch of realism to the JS-2's turret.

this by spraying earth brown on these areas and carrying the color up onto the bow, track fenders, rear hull, and the engine deck. I gave my JS-2's fuel drums rust streaks using thinned brown paint, and I darkened the engine deck grilles with thinned black.

On my model, the cast armor texture on the cupola and turret sides stands out well, **7**. The roof armor is slightly smoother, so the wear on the whitewash is less pronounced. A little extra effort removing the pastel coating is evident around the hatches. I used a moist paintbrush to help expose the vehicle number and make the streaks under the handrails. Black pastel powder was brushed around the turret ventilator.

There you have it: a quick and easy technique for simulating winter camouflage. The result is realistic, and best of all, the process is forgiving. If you make a mistake, you can start over and do it again.

A 1/35 scale Tamiya M3 Stuart before it was weathered with pastels using the author's technique.

BEFORE

Less mess with pastels

Keep pastel dust where it's supposed to be: on your model, not on your hands

BY LEE VANDE VISSE / PHOTOS BY THE AUTHOR

Pastels can be a great material for weathering your models. They are inexpensive, come in a variety of earthy colors, and can be chipped easily with a hobby knife (a No. 10 blade works best) to create dust that's great for simulating mud and crud. However, when brushed straight onto the surface of a model, the dust can pick up fingerprints, shake off, and generally make a mess. Additionally, when pastel dust is oversprayed with a lacquer-based clear flat from an airbrush, much of it is blown away by the blast. You can avoid these problems and take advantage of pastels by following a few simple steps.

AFTER

The Stuart with the patina of a well-used tank thanks to pastel weathering adhered with a careful application of acetone.

ACETONE SAFETY

When using acetone, work only in a well-ventilated area such as a spray booth. Be sure to avoid skin contact, and wear a respirator equipped with the appropriate cartridges.

When your model is ready for weathering, spray it with two or three coats of a lacquer-based clear flat. Let each coat dry before applying the next. Then, use a hobby knife to gently flick the dust onto the appropriate areas of your model. On a tank, for example, you would want to apply the dust around the treads, bogey wheels, and drive sprockets.

Once the dust is in place, use a small paint brush (No. 00 or 000) to transfer acetone to the dust's surface. Use just enough to moisten the dust, and do not actually touch the dust with the brush (just drip the acetone and allow it to seep into the surface). Continue with the rest of the model, and do not move it until you are finished. It's not necessary, but you can apply a final spray of clear flat to seal the entire model.

The magic, of course, is in the acetone, which "wicks" through the dust and dissolves the clear flat beneath. The dissolved clear flat mixes with the pastel dust, so it adheres upon drying. Your dust will now stay where it's supposed to—on your model—and because little is lost through this method, your mud and crud will have a very realistic texture.

MORE TIPS

- Before applying weathering materials, dry-brush your model's high points with a light, contrasting color. This creates the illusion of sunlight on the surface.

- Consider how your subject's operating environment affected weathering. A Sherman tank in the French hedgerows would be coated with dark mud, while a Tiger in North Africa would be covered in light-colored dust.

- If your model will be incorporated into a diorama, make sure the dirt, mud, and dust on the model match the texture and color of those elements in the rest of the diorama.

- If you plan to weather your model with pastels, go easy with airbrushed weathering. Much of what could be accomplished with an airbrush will be added later with the pastel dust.

Weathering an
F-14 MiG KILLER

How to make your Tomcat look like an alley cat

BY DARREN ROBERTS / PHOTOS BY THE AUTHOR

**These days, F-14A Tomcats look pretty grungy.
So how do you dirty up your Cat? Follow Darren's
methods and yours will look awful (or is it good?), too.**

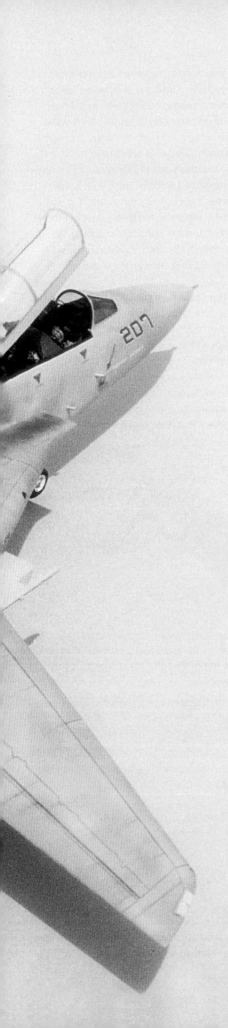

avy aircraft deployed at sea take an absolute beating. Jet exhausts, catapult launches, arrested landings, and corrosion-control maintenance make a jet look like it has been through a 10-round heavyweight fight by the time it returns to shore.

Rarely, if ever, do jets get a fresh coat of paint while out on "the boat." Instead, maintenance crews touch up areas where paint has been chipped or worn off, and sometimes they might not use the correct matching color. This creates a blotchy appearance over the entire aircraft. Add dirt and grime that accumulates during carrier operations, and it turns into a real mess.

I've tried several different ways to recreate this look, and have finally found a method I like. It's a multistep process, but it isn't difficult. Follow along as I dirty up my 1/48 scale Academy Tomcat.

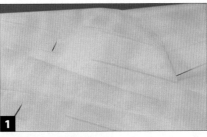

The mottled appearance of current Navy aircraft at sea is mostly due to paint touch-ups. Darren sprayed a lighter shade of gray over the base color to simulate repainted areas.

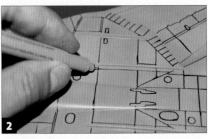

Darren used a technical illustrator's pen to emphasize panel lines.

Excess ink was removed by scouring the surface with fine steel wool.

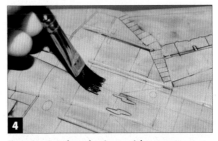

Darren simulated grime with a paste mixture of water and pastel chalk powder.

Step A: Base colors. The first step is to apply the base colors. The Tactical Paint Scheme (TPS) for the Tomcat varies quite a bit from the regulation pattern, and this MiG killer Tomcat from VF-32 "Swordsmen" was no exception. I painted my Tomcat with Testor Model Master Acryl light ghost gray (FS 36375) on the undersurfaces, dark ghost gray (FS 36320) on the anti-glare panel and canopy, and blue gray (FS 35237) on the upper surfaces.

Step B: Corrosion-control touch-ups.
After I finished the base colors, it was time

to simulate some "corrosion control." I studied dozens of Tomcat photos to get a feel for where the majority of maintenance touch-ups were done. In most cases, the repainted areas were lighter than the base color and were concentrated around access panels. I sprayed dark ghost gray touch-ups on the blue gray upper surfaces, **1**, then mixed equal portions of light ghost gray and white to spray the undersurfaces. You can also spray a darker color underneath just for variety. I finished this step by spraying a light mist of Polly Scale dust to add an overall faded appearance.

MiG-KILLER SWORDSMEN

On Jan. 4, 1989, Cmdr. Joseph Connelly (pilot) and Cmdr. Leo Enright (radar intercept officer—RIO) launched on a Combat Air Patrol (CAP) mission from the USS John F. Kennedy patrolling in the Mediterranean off the Libyan coast. They flew an F-14A Tomcat (BuNo 159610) of VF-32 "Swordsmen" and used the call sign Gypsy 207. They and their wingmen received a radar contact from an E-2C Hawkeye indicating that a pair of Libyan aircraft were heading toward the battle group, and it was the Tomcat crews' mission to make sure the Libyans didn't get too close.

Connelly and his wingman engaged the MiG-23 Floggers and locked them on radar, hoping to scare the Libyans away. The MiGs, however, continued on course. Both Tomcats broke left and descended, attempting to get into a better position to escort the MiGs from the area. The MiGs countered this move and continued to approach head-on. Under the rules of engagement, that was considered a hostile move, and Connelly was given permission to fire if needed. Four more times Connelly and his wingman attempted to get in behind the MiGs, and each time the Libyans countered.

Connelly gave Enright permission to arm missiles, and Enright launched two AIM-7 Sparrows, both of which failed to track. Connelly's wingman also launched a Sparrow, which downed one of the MiGs. Connelly got in behind the second MiG and fired an AIM-9 Sidewinder, which impacted behind the cockpit of the Libyan fighter. The Tomcat crews reported seeing two good chutes in the air, but the Libyans were unable to mount a successful search-and-rescue effort.

In the aftermath, Libya claimed that its MiG-23s were unarmed reconnaissance aircraft that were ambushed by 14 enemy planes. However, video footage taken from the television camera system on the F-14 clearly showed that the Floggers were armed with air-to-air missiles, and due to the aggressive nature of the MiGs, the Tomcat pilots were correct in defending the battle group.

Darren Roberts

Step C: Gloss coat. With the touch-up work done, I prepared the model for additional weathering by spraying on a coat of Future acrylic floor polish. The Future formed a barrier to protect the paint from the work I was about to do.

Step D: Panel lines. With the Future completely dry, I ran a .002" Micro Pen through all of the recessed panel lines, **2**. I didn't worry about excess ink outside the lines because it would just be wiped off. I chose the ink pen instead of a wash because it was quicker and less messy.

After finishing with the pen, I removed excess ink on the model with 0000 steel wool, **3**. I lightly scrubbed with steel wool until I was satisfied with the appearance. I applied another coat of Future, and when it was dry, applied the decals.

Step E: Pastel wash/stain. After applying a clear flat coat, I made the fighter look abused.

I ground burnt umber pastel chalk into a small pile of dust, then dipped a wide, soft brush in water, loaded it with pastel dust, and smeared it on the model, **4**. I covered the entire model with the wash, occasionally brushing on clean water to thin it.

I let this wash dry for about 15 minutes, then wiped it off the wash with a wet paper towel and cotton swabs, **5**. If you make a mistake, the pastel dust will come off with water and light scrubbing. When removed, the wash leaves a brownish, dirty-looking stain on the dull coat.

Step F: Surface dirt. To help accentuate the stain, I ground three parts of brown pastel dust and one part black and applied them with a medium-width, stiff-bristle brush to random areas over the entire model, **6**. I concentrated on the underside, as this area gets dirty. I used my thumb to grind the dust into the surface and wipe off excess dust, **7**.

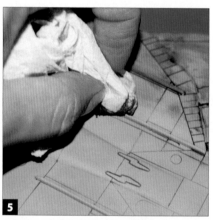

Darren removed excess paste with a moistened paper towel.

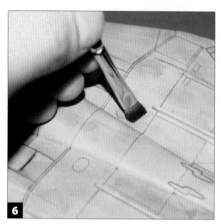

He applied additional stain with a soft brush.

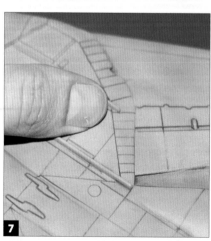

For even more grime, Darren ground the pastel dust into the base paint with his thumb.

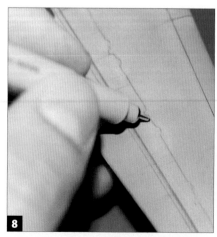

To simulate a lubricant leak, a spot of ink was applied to a likely location.

Step G: Streaks and smudges. I sprayed one more layer of clear flat to seal the pastel dust and to avoid leaving fingerprints in the weathering. I added the canopy, pitot tubes, and engine nozzles, and then set out to work on simulating streaks from lubricant leaks and smudges on heavily used areas.

For hydraulic leaks, I used the Micro Pen to put a small spot of ink where I wanted the streak to start, **8**. I moistened my finger and placed it on the spot, **9**, then pulled back quickly, drawing the ink in the direction I wanted it to go. For larger areas, I used a medium-width, stiff-bristled brush to apply black pastel chalk powder, **10**.

I scrubbed burnt umber pastel powder into the walkways over the air intakes and to the side of the fuselage around the boarding steps, **11**. I used an old round paintbrush with its bristles clipped short.

Now my Tomcat looks right. It looks really bad—in a good way!

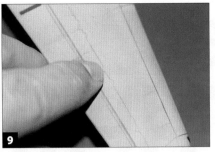
Darren moistened his finger and streaked the ink to simulate the lubricant leak.

He applied wider streaks with a soft brush and black pastel powder.

The heavily soiled walkways were created with burnt umber chalk powder ground in with a stub-bristled brush.

Navy jets rarely look pristine. Tomcats saw constant service, and the elements took their toll.

Extreme
WEATHERING

*Pulling out all the stops to model Revell-Monogram's
SB2C-4 Helldiver as a well-worn Pacific Theater aircraft*

BY JOHN ADELMANN / PHOTOS BY JOHN ADELMANN AND JIM FORBES

**John Adelmann's 1/48 scale Helldiver features "extreme
weathering" techniques. The color scheme is that of an
aircraft based on the USS Essex in April 1945.**

It's a challenge to paint World War II Pacific Theater aircraft, replicating color schemes that look beaten by the elements and abused by the crews. Such extreme weathering involves more than just applying lighter shades of the base color, or daubing a little silver paint here and there.

I used several weathering techniques on Revell-Monogram's ProModeler 1/48 scale SB2C-4 Helldiver (kit No. 5935), with AeroMaster's aftermarket decal sheet (No. 48-204). This "Big-Tailed Beast" flew from the USS Essex in April 1945 and sported the Navy's tricolor camouflage scheme of white, intermediate blue (FS 35164), and nonspecular blue (FS 35042).

Primer. When the assembled Helldiver was free of scratches and dents, I applied Model Master Metalizer non-buffing aluminum plate as a primer coat. After the primer dried, I added several light coats of Future floor polish. I sprayed plenty of Future onto the leading and trailing edges and raised surface detail. The model looked like a shiny quarter, **1**.

Weathering. I applied a coat of Model Master RLM 66 dark gray over all panel lines, **2**. You could get similar results with FS 36118 (gunship gray). Access panels and recessed details such as the rudder and wing flaps got special attention. I painted all panel lines, but I didn't worry about how precisely the paint was laid down, since most of this undercoat would be covered.

Evenly uneven. When the RLM 66 was dry, I mixed some intermediate blue and

1
The Helldiver was primed with Model Master Metalizer nonbuffing aluminum plate and sprayed with several light coats of Future floor polish.

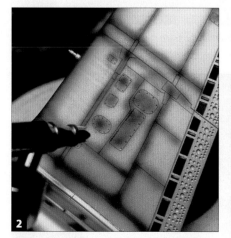

2
John sprayed Model Master RLM 66 on all panel lines, with special attention to access panels and recessed details.

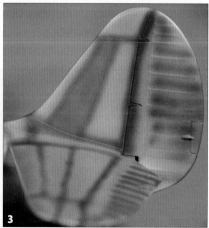

3
The tail surfaces are painted one panel at a time, resulting in what John calls an "evenly uneven" effect.

4 After a coat of intermediate blue, access panel doors on the wing undersides became more noticeable.

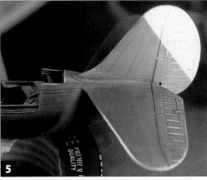

5 Wear on the tail surfaces is simulated by scuffing selected areas down to the primer coat with 2400-grit sandpaper.

6 Rivets and aileron framing showed through after the wing's underside was sanded.

7 Dust specks in the paint are "chipped off" to simulate bare metal. John used a sharpened toothpick to chip paint from panel lines.

8 A wash was applied to recesses. Excess is removed with a damp cloth.

applied it panel by panel. The tail was painted within the confines of the panels, **3**, to create an "evenly uneven" texture that replicated a weathered surface.

When I applied the intermediate blue to the undersides of the wings, the access panel doors became darker and more pronounced, **4**. When the panel lines were filled in, a noticeable weathering effect began to emerge.

Sanding. After the intermediate blue dried, I scuffed the paint surface with a 2400-grit sanding pad until some of the aluminum peeked through, **5**. The coat of Future applied earlier protected the aluminum paint from scratches. The gray rivets at the base of the rudder appeared, the paint on the leading edge was worn away, and the rudder frame looked rather shabby.

Raised rivets on the wing underside access doors appeared nicely after sanding, as did the metal framing on the ailerons, **6**. (The more "bare metal" you want to show, the more you sand; if you remove too much paint, reapply the original color.)

I repeated the painting/sanding process for the underside white and the topside nonspecular blue. I sealed each color with Future so that if I got paint where I didn't want it, I could use thinner to remove it without harming the other colors.

Intentional flaws. When I prepare a model to be painted, I usually remove the sanding dust with a tack cloth and apply a coat of Future to reveal scratches or other imperfections. I did not attempt to remove all the dust from this model—especially on the upper surfaces of the wings—because I used the slightly pebbled surface here and there to help replicate chipped paint.

When I sanded where dust was trapped underneath the paint, tiny specks chipped off, allowing bare metal to show through, **7**. Some model builders press small pieces of masking tape onto the aircraft's surface and quickly remove them, but they run the risk of ripping off too much paint. It's a major sanding project to feather the edges of the chipped paint and/or fill them in with putty.

Rather than risk taking off too much paint, I ran a sharpened toothpick through some of the recessed panel lines, chipping and removing paint as I went. I paid particular attention to the fuselage kick

9

The white portion of the wing "came alive" after the wash was applied.

steps and the access panels that could have been dinged with screwdrivers or other tools during routine maintenance.

Decal/wash prep. After all three colors were applied and sanded, I removed dust from the model and laid down heavier coats of Future. This was perfect surface preparation for the decals and for the wash that was applied to the recesses (removed with a damp cloth after it dried), **8**.

The wash made the white section come alive, **9**, and the AeroMaster decals went on without a hitch, thanks to the slick, smooth surface. I sealed the decals with a final coat or two of Future, which deepened the colors and revealed the underlying shading, **10**. Then I applied several light coats of Model Master acrylic clear flat to bring down the shine.

Extreme weathering takes a little extra effort, but I think the results are worth it. Give it a try on your next model.

10

John gave the Helldiver a coat of Future after decals were in place, then sprayed several light coats of Model Master clear flat to bring down the shine.

This '70 Chevelle looks really bad—which is just what Swedish modeler Anders Isaksson wanted. In this photoessay, he tells how he took it from factory-fresh to road-weary.

Rusty weather

Wearing out AMT/Ertl's 1970 Chevelle SS

BY ANDERS ISAKSSON

Realistic weathering gives a model that final bit of realism and some extra personality—it's my favorite part of scale modeling. Though I build mostly armor and aircraft, every once in a while I build something completely different to try a new technique or just see how a certain idea turns out in reality. Here, I wanted to see whether I could create realistic wear and tear—in the form of rust, dents, and faded paint—on an ordinary car.

It's important to consider how wear occurs on the real thing. Rust holes wouldn't show up on top of road dust, so it's important that the weathering is done in the same order as it would have showed on the real car—apply the weathering from the inside and work your way out.

The kit Anders choose for this project was AMT/Ertl's 1/25 scale 1970 Chevrolet Chevelle SS 454. Since its chromed wheels looked a bit out of place on this car, he substituted the wheels from AMT/Ertl's 1962 Chevrolet Bel Air.

INTERIOR

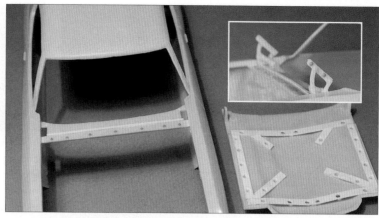

Since I wanted to concentrate on the exterior, it took only a few minutes to put the interior together. I assembled and airbrushed the interior using Tamiya paints mixed in two different shades of dark gray. Small dashboard details were picked out with a small brush in Humbrol black and silver. The only detailing was a Verlinden road map on the dash. An overall dusting with yellow pastels finished my work on the interior.

I added a few simple details to the engine compartment, using a combination of styrene and artistic license. The inside of the hood looked a bit plain, so I built a simple framework from styrene strips and detailed it with drilled holes. Next, I robbed the hinges from the 1962 Chevrolet Bel Air kit (inset), detailed them with a couple of Grandt Line rivets, and glued them in place.

BODYWORK

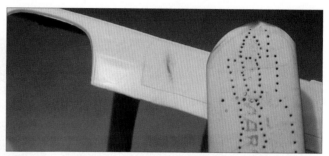

An old, beat-up car should have some dents on it, so I lit a candle and heated a few areas where damage would be likely to appear: front and rear fenders, the front bumper, the driver's door, and the trunk. Be careful not to let the body come too close to the candle. If this happens, the plastic will start crumbling and lose its shape. This technique is a bit difficult to control, and it's a good idea to practice first on a scrap model.

When the plastic gets soft, use a suitable object to make the dent; I prefer an eraser. A finger may leave a print in the soft plastic—not very realistic! Make sure the dents won't interfere with the fit of the chassis and interior. A few molded features, such as the "SS" behind each front wheel, were sanded off, and holes were drilled in their places to give the impression of missing emblems.

BORN TO RUST

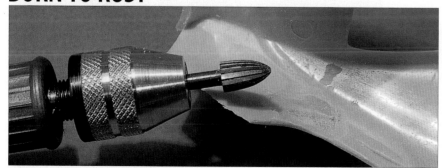

Next I began making the rust holes. The first step is to give the plastic a scale thickness in the areas where the rust will appear, which is done with the help of a motor tool. A small grinder was used to thin the plastic at appropriate places around the inside of the body, mostly in the areas surrounding the wheels.

Using the grinder at a low speed to prevent melting the plastic, I slowly worked my way through. Don't let the grinder go all the way through the plastic—this results in holes that often are too large, with unrealistic soft edges.

When the plastic is thin enough, cut through it with a knife. Avoid giving the holes straight edges when cutting. An irregular outline is important to achieve the illusion of rust slowly eating its way through the metal.

Try to make holes of different sizes, mixing large holes with small ones for greater realism. I continued making rust holes in the area around the wheel until I obtained the rusty look I wanted.

PAINTING

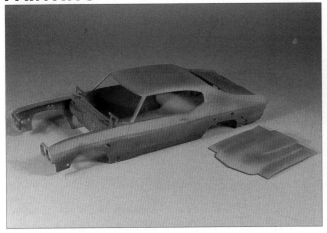

When I was satisfied with my rust holes, I painted the body. I airbrushed Tamiya matte red mixed with a small amount of matte black for a deep red color. I also added a few drops of Tamiya clear, resulting in a slight semigloss finish. When the body had dried, it was misted with a mixture of Tamiya matte red and matte white to make the paint look aged and faded.

I used Humbrol matte dark earth mixed with black oil color for painting the rust holes. Varying the amount of black produces different shades of rust. The rust color was mixed with baking powder to give it a little texture. Some more rust color and baking powder was used in and around the dents, the lower body, and the doors. I finished by lightly dry-brushing the entire body using the rust color (without the baking powder).

I concentrated on the upper surfaces as well as on corners and other areas where the original paint is likely to wear off. I hand-painted the window trim and door handles with Humbrol silver. When this was dry, I finished with a single coat of Gunze Sangyo matte clear to make the trim look dull.

ENGINE

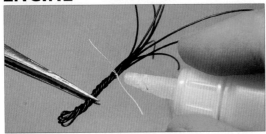

Since I wanted to show my car with the hood open I realized that some extra engine details were needed. The problem: I live in Sweden, so I don't know what a typical American V-8 looks like in real life. When looking at pictures of other car engines I decided to add the ignition wiring from the distributor to the spark plugs. Eight pieces of thin electrical wire were twined and tied together with a piece of sewing thread. I secured the knot with super glue.

After the glue had set, I cut away the surplus below the knot and glued the wiring to the engine in place of the kit distributor. Each wire was painted matte black, then carefully cut to the correct length and glued to the engine. I suspect that I attached the wires too high up on the engine block, each one sitting just below the valve cover, but I found this to be the best spot for gluing each wire. With the engine installed, this error won't be too noticeable.

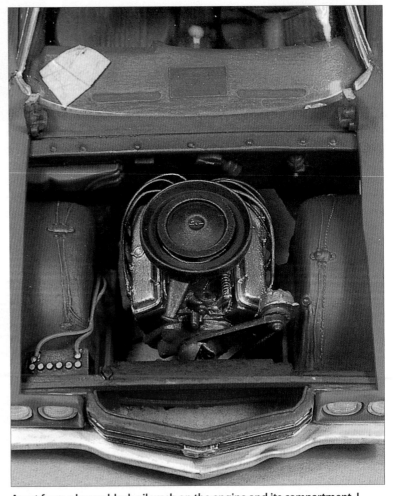

Apart from a heavy black oil wash on the engine and its compartment, I decided to leave the engine alone until final assembly. All that remained was to glue the battery in place together with short pieces of Verlinden flexible tubing for battery cables.

TIRED OUT

The tires need a little work to look good. When they're right out of the box they just look too shiny and new, and each tire has an unrealistic mold line running along the center of the tread.

Removing the mold line required careful cutting with a sharp knife along the tread. After getting rid of the mold line, I sanded down each tire with fine sandpaper to take off the shine.

I gave each tire a light coat of dust consisting of heavily diluted Tamiya matte khaki, making sure that the paint settled in the deep areas of the tread pattern.

Then I sanded the thread surface once again, resulting in a realistic-looking worn tire with dirt collected in the cavities of the tread. Now it was time to put everything together.

FINAL ASSEMBLY

All windows were installed and the chassis was joined to the body. The chromed front and rear bumpers were lightly dry brushed with the rust color and sprayed with Gunze Sangyo matte clear to make them look dull and aged. The grille received a black oil wash to emphasize its pattern.

Both bumpers were glued in place and the hood was attached to its hinges. It was time for the final stage of weathering: road dust. I once again used heavily diluted Tamiya matte khaki, spraying very light on the upper parts of the body, with a little heavier coat around the lower portions, as well as the whole underside of the chassis. The inside of the engine compartment also received a light dusting.

Finally the wheels were glued in place and my Chevelle was complete, looking just as interesting and exciting (to me, at least) as any highly polished show car!

Anything missing? Well, yes. At the end of this project I realized that the kit was lacking a pair of windshield wipers. I guess the owner of this car will have to rely on alternative transportation when the weather gets bad.

Painting Tamiya's
FAIREY
SWORDFISH

Improve a good kit with a great finish

BY JUAN MANUEL VILLALBA / PHOTOS BY THE AUTHOR

It appears that Tamiya's 1/48 scale Fairey Swordfish is nearly faultless. Add Tamiya's photoetched metal detail set to it, and you can't ask for more detail. So, how can you improve an already outstanding kit?

Translating all that miniature detail into a model that looks like the real thing requires a realistic finish. That's the mission here. I painted the floatplane version of the Tamiya kit, airbrushing shadows and highlights to add visual depth to all the details.

The following photostory shows how I went about painting my Swordfish, but the techniques can be used on any color scheme and any model.

This chapter will show you how a couple of expert modelers employ finishing techniques on simply stunning models. These folks have been modeling for some time, so heed the wisdom of the ages.

Tamiya's 1/48 scale Fairey Swordfish floatplane is a state-of-the-art rendition of the famous Royal Navy Fleet Air Arm torpedo bomber. With the separate photoetched metal detail set, there's not much that can be done to make the model look better—so I was obliged to give it a good paint job.

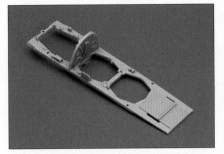 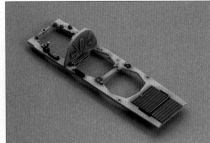

The 27-part cockpit is the most detailed subassembly of Tamiya's kit. The overall color inside was British interior gray-green, and I mixed that using Tamiya acrylics. After it had dried for a day, I washed the parts with a mixture of thinned black and brown oil paint. When that was dry, I dry-brushed with a lightened version of the base coat. Finally, I airbrushed soft shadows to add depth. The photo on the left shows the raw plastic; the photo on the right shows the painted cockpit tub.

The radio gear and the main instrument panel were painted black, and the dials and details carefully added with acrylics. Once the paint was dry, I applied tiny drops of clear gloss to simulate the glass covers for each gauge.

The only additions I made to the cockpit were seat harnesses cut from lead foil, with buckles fashioned from soft wire. The photo on the right shows the seats after painting. I used the same painting routine that I used on the interior parts.

THE FAIREY SWORDFISH

At first glance, the Fairey Swordfish looked antiquated, even by World War II-era standards. It was a lumbering biplane, barely capable of 200 knots (230 mph). Despite its apparent obsolescence, the Swordfish was arguably the most successful—or at least the most celebrated—torpedo bomber of the war. Its legendary victories against the Italian fleet at Taranto and against the German battleship Bismarck are well known, but less well known is that the Swordfish was the first Fleet Air Arm aircraft to sink a submarine in WWII (U-64 on April 13, 1940).

The Swordfish may have been slow, but that proved to be an asset when it came to landing on a carrier in the stormy Atlantic. Slow airspeed also aided in accurately sighting torpedo attacks.

The "Stringbag," as many of its crews dubbed it, was so popular and suitable for its task that it saw service all the way through the war—even longer than its supposed successor, the Fairey Albacore.

Although designed and initially produced by Fairey, all but 692 of the 2,391 Swordfish were produced by Blackburn. The last Swordfish was retired June 28, 1945, more than two months after Germany's surrender. That day marked the last flight of a biplane in Britain's Fleet Air Arm.

Paul Boyer

The finished cockpit fit well into the fuselage. I used brown paint to simulate the leather pads on the cockpit sills.

The Swordfish's engine had an exhaust collector ring incorporated into the front of the cowl. I painted the cylinder banks satin black, then dry-brushed them with flat aluminum. I painted the exhaust collector ring flat aluminum first, then applied light coats of brown, thinned with eight parts of thinner to two parts of paint. Tamiya's photoetched metal detail set includes the bracing that holds the cowling in place.

The photoetched metal set includes all the rigging wires, which are made to fit into predrilled holes. I think the best way to install each wire is to glue one end, bend the shaft gently, and let the other end rest in its hole. The strange-looking black items with the graduated white posts are lead-sighting devices for aiming torpedoes at enemy ships. Note the red tie-down ring at the strut attachment post.

The metal areas on the real Swordfish were painted gray, while aluminum dope was used on the fabric coverings. I painted gray on the forward fuselage, floats, lower rear fuselage, center section of the upper wing, and the interplane struts. I dry-brushed a soft coat of slightly lighter gray around the panel lines, and soft brown on the floats. I accented all the panel lines with a pencil before sealing the finish with a clear satin coat.

The fabric sections were next. Here I used Tamiya X11 chrome silver; it's easy to apply and looks like aluminum dope. To accent the panel lines, I applied a diluted mixture of acrylic black and brown with a 00 brush. Capillary action drives the paint through the lines. When the wash was dry, I polished all the aluminum areas with a cotton ball.

I painted the torpedo satin black, then lightly dry-brushed the propeller and fins with Tamiya gunmetal. The area around the tailhook was metal on the real Swordfish, so I painted it gray. Control wires to the elevator and rudder were made from monofilament.

Modeling Ike Kepford's
CORSAIR

Scott Murphy transforms Revell's "fixer upper" into a showpiece

BY SCOTT MURPHY / PHOTOS BY THE AUTHOR

Revell's 1/32 scale F4U-1A Corsair was a state-of-the-art kit when first released in 1970. It had a decent engine, detailed cockpit, and moveable wings that could be posed open or folded. But by today's standards the kit is Spartan—in real estate terms, it would be classified as a "fixer upper." The potential for a beautiful model is there, but the modeler has to exert extra effort.

I decided to use this kit to model the F4U-1A of Navy Lt. Ira "Ike" Kepford as it appeared when he was based on Bougainville in 1944. Kepford was the top-scoring ace (16 confirmed kills) of VF-17, the famous Jolly Rogers squadron. I was fortunate to have an example of a real Corsair at the National Museum of Naval Aviation in Pensacola as a constant reference. I also used Detail & Scale's book on the Corsair.

I realized much of the model would have to be rebuilt. Rather than build all the new detail from scratch, I decided to use aftermarket resin parts. As it turned out, a lot of scratchbuilding was still necessary to improve the resin items and add small details. Even with the resin parts, this project was going to require creativity.

It may be an old player, but Revell's 1/32 scale Corsair isn't out of the game yet. With resin detail parts and some scratchbuilding, Scott Murphy turned it into a winner.

While Revell's cockpit may have been acceptable when the kit was first issued, it needed to be brought up to modern standards. Scott replaced the original cockpit with a resin detail set from Lone Star.

Scott supplemented Lone Star's cockpit with instruments and a placard set from Waldron. The gun sight still needed work, so he added more detail made from styrene sheet and rod.

Even the canopy was thoroughly detailed with scratchbuilt cranks, mirrors, cables, and hand-holds.

MODEL AT A GLANCE

The foundation of Scott Murphy's Corsair is Revell's old 1/32 scale F4U-1A. Scott detailed his model with aftermarket resin parts. He added a resin engine from Teknics (a kit in itself!) and replaced the kit's cockpit, wheel wells, flaps, and wheels with parts from Lone Star. The instruments and placard set in the cockpit are from Waldron (no longer produced).

Scott improved the resin parts and added more detail by scratchbuilding additional parts, including the landing gear. The model was painted with Testor Model Master enamels and weathered with Metalizer, pastels, and "The Detailer" wash thinned with Future floor polish.

Cockpit. I replaced the cockpit with Lone Star's resin detail set, **1**. Then I added Waldron's instruments and placard set. I scratchbuilt additional switches, levers, knobs, and a gun sight mount from wire and styrene, **2**.

The gun sight needed more details, so I made them from styrene sheet and rod. To simulate optics, I turned a piece of clear sprue in my motor tool until it was the correct diameter and had a curved surface. Then I inserted it in the top of the sight. I also added both reflector glasses (one tinted yellow), but in checking my references, I discovered Kepford's aircraft had the reflectors mounted on the windscreen. I removed the reflector glasses and attached the windscreen glass. I added cranks, mirrors, hand-holds, and actuating cables to the canopy, **3**, and the attachment points for the gun sight glass to the windscreen.

Engine, cowling, propeller, and oil cooler. The kit's Pratt & Whitney R-2800 engine had some glaring inaccuracies, including poorly shaped cylinders and incorrect magnetos. Grinding off the inaccurate parts and making replacements from scratch would have been a major undertaking.

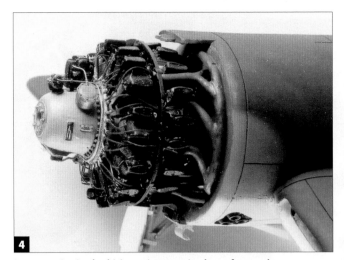

4

Inaccuracies in the kit's engine required an aftermarket replacement: Teknics' resin R-2800 engine. Scott still had to scratchbuild the ignition ring, wiring, and pushrods.

5

The cooling flaps on the kit's cowling were replaced with more accurate ones made from soda-can aluminum. Scott also added the actuating gear under the flaps.

6

The kit's oil cooler inlets were replaced with new ones made from styrene sheet and strip and brass screen. Just to the left of the inlet, you can see the engine exhaust stubs, made from aluminum tube.

7

A lot of carefully formed brass, steel, aluminum, wire, and styrene went into the new scratchbuilt main gear struts.

Instead, I chose the superb Teknics R-2800 resin engine kit, **4**. The detail is crisp, and the kit includes the correct magnetos. I scratchbuilt the ignition ring, wiring, and pushrods. The front and rear rows of cylinders are separated by a ring that was not included in the Teknics kit. I used the one from the original kit; the fit was nearly perfect. I shortened the back of the engine with my motor tool and a cutting bit so it would fit correctly in the kit's cowling.

Revell's cowling had the wrong number of cooling flaps, and they were the wrong shape, thickness, and configuration. I ground them off, replaced them with soda-can aluminum, and added the actuating pulleys and wires, **5**. I made the internal ribs and stringers from strip styrene. The finished cowling contained nearly 200 pieces of styrene, aluminum, and wire. It was a lot of work, but the result was worth it.

Because opening the engine compartment cooling vent created a "black hole" on the underside of the fuselage, I filled the space with a small box made from styrene. It didn't seem worth the effort to scratchbuild the engine mounts, exhaust system, and wiring just for this one vent. I made the exhaust stubs out of

aluminum tube, and I punched out discs from styrene sheet for the carburetor blow-off vents.

The kit's propeller blade and spinner were correctly shaped. I added details to the hub, made from styrene rod and strip.

The oil cooler inlets in the wing roots were poorly represented, so I scratchbuilt new ones from brass screen and styrene strip and sheet, **6**. I added a large strip of styrene to the top of the wing where it meets the fuselage to correct a ⅛" gap.

Since I had opened the cowling's cooling flaps, the back of the engine was visible. Before attaching the finished cowling to the aircraft, I mounted the engine on the firewall and scratchbuilt the exhaust headers from .10" solder. Unfortunately, most of this work ended up concealed under the cowling.

Landing gear, wheel wells, and bomb rack. The kit's landing gear was the wrong size and lacked detail, so I scratchbuilt replacements. I made the model's tail wheel strut from styrene and the main gear struts from brass, steel, aluminum, wire, and styrene. I made the bracing and actuating cylinders from styrene. The landing gear is as close to scale as my eyes and calipers would permit, **7**.

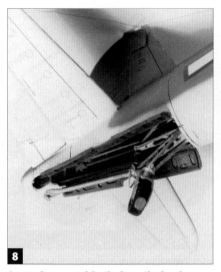

8 Scott also scratchbuilt the tail wheel assembly and hook. He made the wheel from a segment of ½" acrylic rod.

9 A Brewster bomb rack completes the underside. The original was crudely made, so Scott's job of copying it was easy.

10 Scott replaced the kit's flaps with resin ones from Lone Star, which allowed him to pose them in the dropped position. He still had to scratchbuild the bulkheads inside the panels.

11 The wingtip navigation light didn't escape Scott's attention. It's made from a piece of acrylic rod ground and sanded to shape.

The tail hook was scratchbuilt from styrene and a piece of scrap resin, and the tail wheel was fabricated from a piece of ½" clear acrylic rod, **8**.

I replaced the kit's wheel wells and doors with more Lone Star resin parts. I added plumbing for the hydraulics, but little else needed to be done. Bridle hooks were made from brass rod; aluminum and solder served for the drain lines and the Brewster bomb rack's attachment point.

Brewster bomb racks were used widely during 1944, so I decided to scratchbuild one for my model, **9**. The real thing was rather crude, which made my job pretty easy.

Control surfaces. The flaps on a Corsair are difficult to model, so I used Lone Star's outstanding resin flaps, **10**. This saved a lot of time compared with modifying the kit's flaps, which were woefully inadequate. The bulkhead behind them is curved rather than flat because the flaps were the Fowler type that rotated

outward as well as downward. This would be easy to do on a straight wing, but the gull wing complicates things.

I started with a flat bulkhead but added a piece of .125" x .125" styrene strip hollowed with a circular motor tool bit. I worked the strip into final shape by sanding and filling with super glue. The flaps were attached after painting, and hinges were added. Styrene sheet simulates the spring-loaded plates that swing up toward the flaps when they are extended.

The kit contains clear parts for the wingtip navigation lights, but they fit poorly. I cut a piece of acrylic rod and drilled a hole to simulate the bulb, then glued it in place. I used a motor tool, files, and sandpaper to shape and polish it, **11**. The formation lights in the wings were made from clear pieces of styrene punched out with a Waldron punch set and painted with Gunze clear colors. A piece of punched aluminum foil was placed in the hole before the styrene to make the colors stand out.

With its aftermarket detail and scratchbuilt extras, Scott updated the Revell kit into a striking model of Lt. Kepford's Corsair.

Finishing. The model was primed and painted with Testor Model Master enamels in the tricolor paint scheme used on Kepford's plane. The kit decals had deteriorated with age and disintegrated as soon as solvent was applied. Fortunately, I had anticipated this and scanned them at 1200 dpi before beginning construction. I printed them out, made masks from packing tape, and hand painted the national insignia.

The Jolly Rogers insignia and the white "29" are from white decal film. The stroke of the kit's "29" decals was too thick, so I made a set of templates on my computer using the "Amarillo USAF" font (available at www.tlai.com). I used Archer dry transfers and homemade decals for the stenciling.

Weathering. The South Pacific was not kind to aircraft. I used crushed coral from Guam on the base, and it's easy to see why paint didn't hold up well out there—the stuff is extremely abrasive. My reference photos showed the outer third of Kepford's prop nearly devoid of paint. The leading edges of

the wings and stabilizers had numerous chips in them. I hand-painted the chips with Testor aluminum Metalizer. The most difficult part was simulating the wear on the top of the wing near the fuselage. Even though the rivet heads were flush, they took the brunt of the wear. I nearly went blind painting dots!

I applied pastels to the upper surfaces to "fade" the paint and simulate soot from the exhausts and guns.

Radial engines are notorious oil leakers. "The Detailer" brown wash (mixed from red, yellow, and black) and Future simulate oil stains. I placed a drop on the area and blew on it slowly and steadily to spread it out. If you do this carefully, you can get the "oil" to flow as if it were spread by the slipstream.

To simulate doped paper placed over the gun ports and shell ejection chutes (a measure to prevent gun jamming), I cut pieces from white address labels and covered these areas.

There you have it: a Plain Jane model that became an accurate, detailed representation of Ike Kepford's war-weary Corsair.

Techniques

Readers and editors of *FineScale Modeler* magazine can help you solve dozens of finishing foibles and technique troubles.

Tips

☐ Blow away that dust

After many hours of research, building, and painting, your fine model sits on a shelf to be admired—and attacked by annoying dust.

But dust can be blown away by a trip to your local photography shop to purchase a blower brush. It gently brushes dust away, and squeezing the bulb delivers a soft gust of air to dislodge dust in those hard-to-reach areas, such as struts and wires on biplanes.

George Zupko
San Rafael, California

■ Talc for texture

Rusty metal tends to have a rough surface and to "bubble" through paint. Add some talcum powder to your rust paint to thicken it and give it texture. The talc lightens the paint considerably, so add some black or dark brown to the mix or apply a second coat of rust.

To show the rust breaking through the paint in patches, dry brush the base color over the rust-treated areas.

Paul Adams
Auckland, New Zealand

■ Burnished graphite

To simulate darkened, polished-metal surfaces, paint the applicable areas with gloss white, chrome silver, or very light gray from Testor, depending on the desired effect. After a day or two, apply some finely ground graphite powder with a small brush. Use a finger to gradually burnish the graphite into the surface.

If the effect is too heavy, wash with soapy water; if it's too light, add more graphite. When you are satisfied with the

depth and luster, seal with Future acrylic floor polish for a long-lasting sheen.

Ronald Elsdoerfer
Warwick, Rhode Island

■ If it's good enough for hair . . .

Try treating your good-quality natural-bristle paint brushes with some hair shampoo/conditioner. This will help keep the bristles soft and prevent them from becoming dried and brittle from age and repeated cleaning in solvent.

Wet the bristles with water and apply a small amount of shampoo/conditioner between your thumb and forefinger. Work into the brush from the base of the bristles to the tip for about a minute, then rinse in warm running water, stroking the bristles to remove all of the treatment.

Note: Because most solvents and water don't mix, allow a solvent-cleaned brush to dry thoroughly before using this technique.

Mark Johnston
Temple City, California

☐ Look, Mom, no scratches!

When removing scratches from clear plastic, you'll get better results by polishing in straight lines rather than in circular patterns. Polish in one direction with fine wet-or-dry sandpaper, then at 90 degrees to the first with the next finer grade. Alternate directions as you work down to your finest grade of sandpaper.

Circular polishing reinforces the small scratches from the previous grade of paper. Polishing in straight lines and alternating directions removes the coarser abrasion marks and replaces them with finer ones.

Jonathan Davies
Milton Keynes, England

■ Erase the problem

Despite my efforts to mask properly before painting, I still occasionally get fuzzy edges or paint buildup. Here's my trick for fixing the problem: after removing the masking tape, I let the paint dry overnight. The next day, I clean up the edge using a soft vinyl drafting eraser (the Staedtler Mars No. 526-50 works well), available at stores that sell drafting, engineering, or art supplies.

I cut the eraser into small wedges and literally erase away the fuzz and buildup. No repainting, no touch up, no mess—and it's fast. With a little care, a ridge can be reduced

☐ = Before painting; ■ = Painting; ■ = After painting